To President

Stephen D. Livesay , Ph.D.

Bryan College

From   Dr. Young-Gil Kim

Founding President

Handong Global University

Pohang, Korea

Why Not Transform The World?
From Entropy to Syntropy

Syntropy Drama

"Syntropy is the phenomenon in which nature moves towards order, organization and life which is the opposite of Entropy. Syntropy refers to the supernatural restoration of God's created order of spirituality, morality, and eternal life."

Syntropy Drama

1st Edition, June 2014
2nd Printing, July 2014
Published by Duranno International Ministry
Phone : 213-382-5400
Email : duranno@duranno.us
Homepage : www.duranno.us
Address : 616 S. Westmoreland Ave. Los Angels, CA 90005.

"신트로피 드라마"
By Kim, Young-Gil

Copyright@2013 by Duranno Press
Originally published in Korea by Duranno Press

All Scripture quotations, unless otherwise indicated, are taken from the Holy Bible, New International Version.

Printed in the USA

ISBN 978-0-692-23804-2

Why Not Transform the World?
From Entropy to Syntropy

Syntropy Drama

Dr. Young-Gil Kim

Duranno

CONTENTS

PART ONE

The Law of Syntropy I Faith, the Assurance of Things Not Seen _37

Recommendations

"*Syntropy Drama* is an amazing story of the way God's power and grace works through individuals and institutions. Dr. Young-Gil Kim offers a compelling autobiographical testimony of his intellectual and spiritual journey from atheistic naturalism to life changing commitment to Jesus Christ. Whether writing of his own faith journey or the origins, development, and fruits of Handong Global University, Dr. Kim attests boldly to the providential hand of God in the course of his tenure as president. This book is an inspiring testimony for those of us privileged to work faithfully within Christian academic institutions."

Michael K. Le Roy

President

Calvin College

Grand Rapids, Michigan

"Syntropy manifests itself in acts of redemption and creation. In this book, Dr. Young-Gil Kim articulates his own personal redemption and that of his family and then goes on to share the amazing story of building Handong Global University, in Pohang, Korea. As one who has been involved in building a college in New York City, I was greatly encouraged by his words. The book is personal, warm, and ultimately the story of God at work through the lives of faithful people. It is a quick read, but an important example for today's followers of Christ."

Andy Mills

Former Chairman and President

The King's College

New York City

"From the mountains of South Korea and the miracle of Handong Global University comes this important truth: those of us in Christian education have been called to the holy task of transformation. We are a part of God's redeeming work."

Dale A Lunsford
President
LeTourneau University
Longview, Texas

"It is an honor to have an early insight in this inspiring book by Dr. Young-Gil Kim, founding chartered president of Handong Global University. He shares his testimony wrapped within the dynamics between entropy (increasing "natural" disorder) and syntropy (supernatural, God-given restoration) of the fallen world. Leading Handong Global University through the first critical years since 1995 towards a globally respected and high-standing institution, Dr. Kim was shaped to become a unique role-model of Christian leadership for today's world. Proverbs 11:28 (Msg) ("A life devoted to things is a dead life, a stump; a God-shaped life is a flourishing tree") is an appropriate summary of this message, which I strongly recommend both to Christians and non-believers."

Wilhelm Holzapfel

Honorary Professor for Industrial Microbiology

Technical University of Karlsruhe (KIT), Germany

Invited Chair Professor

Handong Global University, Korea

"Dr. Young-Gil Kim's new book, *Syntropy Drama*, is the uplifting tale of one man's journey from atheist scientist to devout Christian and founding president of Handong Global University (HGU). Dr. Kim's life has in many ways been a difficult one, as he chronicles in this book, and the lessons he learned are embodied in the ideals of HGU, "God's university." The 21st century is the age of speed and collaboration across boundaries. The proper mission of higher education in today's world is encapsulated in HGU's twin mottos, "Study to Give to Others" and "Why Not Change the World?" Dr. Kim's story is an inspiring one, and his book is a must-read blueprint for understanding how Christianity and higher education can transform our shared world for the better."

Toyoshi Satow

President

International Association of University Presidents (IAUP)

Chancellor

J. F. Oberlin University, Tokyo, Japan

"It is my hope that all Christians living in the 21st century read this book. To me, Dr. Kim's life story seems to have overlapping similarities to the early Christians in the New Testament. The apostle Paul wrote, "Join together in following my example, brothers and sisters, and just as you have us as a model, keep your eyes on those who live as we do." (Philippians 3:17 NIV) I believe that Dr. Kim is truly a man of God and example in faith to us. Through this book, the readers will not only learn the difference between the humanistic and Christian world view, but also gain insight into the stance we must take as Christians. Furthermore, *Syntropy Drama* gives us hope in our Christian walk. Handong Global University, in which Dr. Kim served as founding president, vision statement "Why Not Change the World?" reminds the students and faculty of their individual purpose and mission in life. Dr. Kim ends the book with the statement which focuses on regaining our spiritual purpose as

the key for living in the 21st century. May God's glory be evident to all through this book."

Usami Minoru

Chairman of Genesis

Japan

"In the age we live in, the saying "It is hard for scientists to believe in God" has almost been accepted as the norm. However, through Dr. Young-Gil Kim, a former atheist and NASA scientist, and his book *Syntropy Drama*, God has shown me that "Scientists actually believe in God in a deeper and more straight-forward fashion than others." Day to day, people witness and rely on natural laws, but make little effort in seeking the Maker of these laws. Dr. Kim, not only met our Maker, but also was able to experience new laws and truths of God. These experiences are the backbone of this book amply named *Syntropy Drama*. To the people today who are well versed in the Law of Entropy, this book has shown people that the Law of Syntropy exists. It is my prayer that everyone who reads this book will experience their own version of Syntropy Drama."

Jae-Hoon Lee

Senior Pastor

Onnuri Presbyterian Church

Seoul, Korea

Acknowledgment

For the publication of this book *Syntropy Drama* in English, I have received incredible support from my Christian brothers and sisters in Korea and around the world.

I would especially like to express my utmost gratitude to Mrs. Dalleen Lee Hah (wife of the late founder and senior pastor of Onnuri Presbyterian Church, Dr. Yong-Jo Hah). Without her prayers, encouragement and support, *Syntropy Drama* would have never materialized.

Also I would like to express my sincerest thanks to:

• Handong Global University (HGU) President Soon Heung Chang, Ph.D., whom I have no doubt that God will bless and lead HGU to His will;

• HGU's professors, faculty, staff, students, and alumni;

• Professor Nicholas Scott Lantinga, of the School of International Studies, Language & Literature of HGU, and his wife Sherrin for their assistance editing this manuscript;

• Rev. Samuel Y. Hwang, Esq., for review and editing;

• Bernice Choi, for the initial translation;

• OprahYouljin Lee and StellaYuna Jeong, secretaries at HGU, and Momin Kim, for their help;

• Sarah K. Yoon, for her comprehensive review and final editing;

• E wan for the cover and Sun-Hee Kim for editing of this book;

• Duranno USA and Mr. Sung-Suk Hah, for publishing the English version of *Syntropy Drama*.

Furthermore, I would like to express my deepest thanks and appreciation to Dr. Alvin Austin, former president of LeTourneau University, Longview, Texas and Dr. Gaylon Byker, former president of Calvin College for their prayers during my imprisonment in 2001 related to the HGU's financial difficulties. My appreciation is also extended to Dr. Paul R. Corts, former president of Washington-based International Association of the Council for Christian Colleges & Universities (CCCU) for visiting the HGU campus in order to encourage and develop a close international partnership between CCCU and HGU.

Finally, I would like to thank my beloved wife Phyllis Young-Ae Kim, my son Jimmy Ho-Min Kim, daughter-in-law Jung-Min Lee, grandchildren Claire, Christian and my daughter Joann Jong-Min Kim, son-in-law Joseph Byoung-Hee Park, granddaughters Hannah and Gina for their sincere prayers for publication of this book.

Young-Gil Kim

April 2014

Prologue

Man is created by God and is finite, mortal, and imperfect. Thus, no man is capable of fully comprehending an infinite God. Not only did God create the universe, but providentially governs it by His infinite wisdom, with nothing escaping His attention or control. Yet, man chose a path of sin, separation and destruction. Nonetheless, God provided a way, through the blood of Jesus Christ, to redeem us to be used as God's instruments and to fulfill His special plan.

I often think of God as the master director who guides my life. It is as if I am the star of a drama that unfolds on his stage. As I reflect upon my life, God clearly guided the path upon which I walked even when I could not see or could not have chosen it myself. God took me on a journey from being a NASA scientist to being a professor at the Korea Advanced Institute of Science and Technology (KAIST), and eventually to becoming the founding president of Handong Global University ("Handong" or "HGU"), what I lovingly call, "God's university." In the process, I was awakened to a very special vision God had in mind for Handong for the 21st century.

Leading a brand-new university, however, was no easy task. From the start, Handong experienced un-fathomable financial difficulties, which eventually led to lawsuits and criminal charges against me. In the process, I was imprisoned for 53 days, which were the most difficult time of my life. And yet, they were also the most blessed time of my life, for during this time I would most vividly experience the living God.

The harsh realities in my life would prove time and again the faithfulness of God's promise that "God works for the good of those who love him, and have been called according to His purpose" (Romans 8:28).[1] Through it all, God nurtured the growth of my faith and helped me to clearly understand His heart for Handong.

Years later, not only I, but also the entire Handong community came to a refreshing realization that all of the past trials and troubles were God's way of purifying and establishing Handong as God's university. I am convinced that what happened at Handong was an unfolding of the storyline of a drama written by God.

It has been over 19 years since I responded to the call to serve as Handong's president. In all honesty, I was never able to take a real vacation. I had been incredibly busy because of non-stop administrative, speaking and teaching schedules, even on weekends. Often, I had to travel throughout Korea and overseas to raise the necessary funds to keep Handong financially afloat. In July 2013, I was finally able to take my first real vacation.

During this most precious time of rest, I happened to come upon a copy of *See the Invisible, Change the World*,[2] a testimonial book I had written in 2006. As I flipped through the pages of the book, I reminisced about the numerous miracle-like events that took place at Handong over the years. I immediately sensed that God's providence and grace had always been at work. At about the same time, I also re-read and was touched by Henri Nouwen's book, *In the Name of Jesus: Reflections on Christian Leadership*.[3] Although I had read his book a number of times in the past, it touched my heart in a new way. It caused me to meditate on the heart of Jesus in terms of how he would approach the issue of leadership in the 21st century.

The meditation ended with a deep repentance before God. I realized that during my 19 years of presidency at Handong, I clearly lacked the spiritual discipline of deep meditational prayer, having yielded to the pressures of urgency and busyness in my daily schedule. I also realized that Nouwen and I shared the common experience of being alone over time. I feared, however, that such a feeling could mean that I was spiritually down and depressed. Nouwen emphasized how God-centered prayer, an attitude of humility, and being poor in spirit defined Christian leadership. His words reminded me that I could very well become estranged from God when I do not protect my prayer time.

I became desperate for the deeper meditational prayer that the tyranny of urgency had taken away from me over the years. In the process, I repented not having been humble before God as a leader. God restored me and this book is a result of God's work of restoration in me.

The Syntropy Drama of God!

This book is about an amazingly restorative and redemptive work of God. The Syntropy Drama of God unfolds as His Word goes directly against the currents of the world and brings about stunning transformation to this universe.

The stories in this book form a mosaic—the stories of how an atheist scientist was called to the presidency of God's university; about my personal meditation on God's creation and His laws and the culmination of history; the educational philosophy of Handong; and the 21st century leadership. They may seem unrelated, but together they demonstrate how God restores and redeems His people and His world: a Syntropy Drama of God.

Even today, the Syntropy Drama of God is unfolding in all aspects of life. I begin with my personal life, and then show how it restores and redeems families, communities and societies, nations, and all God's creation from the effects of this world through Christian leadership. In Chapter 3, I will share a story about how the Syntropy Drama has been unfolding on a stage called Handong Global University in Pohang,

South Korea.

Through this short book, I desire to share God's glorious drama as he directed and led me through the journey of my life. In writing this book, my only regret is my own lack of capacity to express more wonderfully what God has done in my life. I would love for this book to be a good guide for atheists-turned-believers in their process of learning more of God. I hope readers would be able to get a glimpse of God's heart for the 21st century leadership.

I pray that the vexatiousness and meaninglessness of life, the conflicts and troubles within humanity, and the injustices and degradations in the world would be restored and redeemed by the life of Christ. Finally, I hope that this book will lead some readers to recognize that God has established each one of us as a star actor in His Syntropy Drama of restoring and redeeming this world from "disorder" to "order."

"But as for me, it is good to be near God. I have made

the Sovereign Lord my refuge; I will tell of all your deeds." (Psalm 73:28)

Young-Gil Kim

July 2013

Montville, New Jersey

Introduction

In Genesis 1, God created the universe and everything in it. God's creation order was perfect, but it was destroyed by the fall (Genesis 3). The First Law of Thermodynamics (the Law of Conservation of Energy) states that energy is a fixed quantity which cannot be created or destroyed, it can only be transformed. When man sinned and betrayed God, all creation became corrupt and caused the material world to deteriorate by going from order to disorder. Therefore, disorder and chaos (entropy) naturally increased. In 1864, Rudolf Clausius, a German physicist, introduced the term "entropy" (from Greek en = diverge, tropos = tendency). He explained the Law of Entropy as a natural process of increasing disorder that occurs in the material world (also known as the Second Law of Thermodynamics).[4]

According to the Law of Entropy, all changes that occur in nature and the material world must collapse, degrade, and decay, thus going from order to disorder over time. For example, metal will rust, smoke will dissipate into the air, rocks will weather into sand, and trees will die and decompose. The fact that perfume molecules disperse into the air when the lid is opened and that an ink drop propagates over water all prove the Law of Entropy. This demonstrates how energy is dispersed with an increasing degree of disorder. Entropy is the tendency towards dissipation of energy, chaos, disorder and death. Entropy is a universal "force" that causes organized forms to gradually disintegrate into lower and lower levels of organization. In other words, it is like the force that causes great machines to eventually run down and wear out.

The Law of Syntropy

Living organisms, however, do not follow the Law of Entropy. In contrast, they become increasingly more systematized and organized throughout the span of their life cycle. In living things, matter and energy concentrate, differentiate, and evolve towards complexity and structure. "Syntropy" describes the opposite phenomenon of entropy which comes from the Greek syntropos (syn = converge, tropos = tendency); it means "to converge the flow of energy." It was coined by an eminent Italian mathematician, Dr. Luigi Fantappiè. The following is a quotation of his own words regarding his new idea of syntropy.

"I have no doubts about the date when I discovered the law of syntropy. It was in the days just before Christmas 1941, when as a consequence of conversation with two colleagues, a physicist and a biologist, I was suddenly projected in a new panorama, which radically changed the vision of science and of the Universe which I had inherited from my teachers and which I had always considered the strong and certain ground on which to base my scientific investigations. Suddenly I saw the possibility of interpreting a wide range of solutions of the wave equation which can be considered the fundamental law of the universe. However, the solutions had been always rejected as "impossible," but suddenly the solutions appeared "possible," and they explained a new category of phenomena which I named "syntropic," totally different from entropic ones, of the mechanical, physical and chemical laws, which obey only the principle of classical causation and the law of entropy···. Scientists finally recognized that syntropic phenomena were real and existed in the living systems in nature···. The properties of the new syntropic law opened consequences which could deeply change the biological, medical, psychological, and social sciences."[5]

This syntropic law was later quoted by Hungarian Dr. Albert Szent-Gyorgyi, who won the Nobel Prize in Physiology for the discovery of vitamin C. He postulated the principle of syntropy which causes living systems to reach "higher and higher levels of organization, order and dynamic harmony."[6] He stated the following:

"It is impossible to explain the qualities of organization and order of living things starting from the entropic laws of the macrocosm. This is one of paradoxes modern biology: the properties of living systems are opposed to the law of entropy that governs the macrocosm. Life always shows a decrease in entropy and increase in complexity, in direct conflict with the law of entropy."

While entropy is a universal law that leads to disintegration of inorganic physical worlds, Dr. Albert Szent-Gyorgyi concluded that syntropy is the universal law of life. Syntropy is constantly being demonstrated and is symmetrical to the law of entropy. But instead of disintegration, syntropy leads living systems towards more and harmonious forms of organization. Dr. Szent-Gyorgyi suggested the existence of a law symmetrical to the law of entropy when he noticed a major difference between amoebas and humans. He observed an increase of complexity that requires the existence of a mechanism that is able to counteract the law of entropy. In other words, there must be a force that is able to counter the universal tendency of matter towards dissipation. Life always shows a decrease in entropy and an increase in complexity, in direct conflict with the law of entropy.

"In the Unified Theory of the Physical and Biological World" by Dr. Luigi Fantappiè, he found that syntropy and entropy constantly interact in nature.[7] The syntropic processes of concentration of matter and energy cannot be definite, and entropic processes are needed to compensate syntropic concentration. This tells us that when entropy goes down syntropy rises, and when entropy rises syntropy goes down. Consequently, the visible reality of entropy can directly affect the invisible reality of syntropy. Entropy is the tendency towards disorder, dissipation, corruption, suffering, and death, whereas syntropy is the tendency towards order, cohesion, well-being, harmony and life. Because the total energy in the universe is a fixed quantity, the sum of entropic energy (diverging) and syntropic energy (converging) is constant and complementary. The law of complementarity suggests that if we want to increase syntropy (well-being), we just have to lower entropy.[8] Entropic energies tend to contaminate the physical environment and destroys life by creating psychological and existential suffering of depression, anxiety, stresses, tensions, and lack of meaning of life. Survival of our happy life depends on our ability to reduce entropy and increase syntropy. For syntropic physical health, the material needs of right foods, clean water and air, and sunlight, etc. are essential. For the invisible syntropic aspects of moral, ethical, and spiritual lives, the immaterial needs of love, fellowships, hope, and faith are vital.

The ultimate purpose of Syntropy Drama is to transform the world from a natural entropic disorder of chaos to God's supernatural syntropic order of restoration by the power of Holy Spirit in every aspect of spirituality, morality, and eternal life.

"The Spirit gives life; the flesh counts for nothing."
(John 6:63)

"'Behold, I will create new heavens and a new. The former things will not be remembered, nor will they come to mind.'" (Isaiah 65:17)

When the world was created in the beginning as in Genesis 1, the syntropy (created order) was perfect, and entropy (disorder) was non-existent. Since the Man's Fall due to sin, we see entropy not only in the material world, but also in various areas of society as we observe breakdowns in politics, economy, and cultures as well as in individuals, families and even the church. Yet, God desires to transform the fallen creation and bring restoration and redemption. For this purpose, God sent His only Son, Jesus Christ, to this earth. God is calling us, as Christians, to be His agents to carry out His restoration and redemptive plan.

God desires a transformation of this world. To be

transformed, there must a renewing of our minds, going from self-centered thinking to God-centered thinking. A transformation of this fallen world will not occur until and unless humanity decides to abandon the laws of gravitation and greed. Such laws only promote more power, more money and more fame for egocentric purposes. Instead, the laws of God's grace must be pursued, which promotes the interests of others.[9] And the laws of God's grace are best demonstrated by Jesus Christ.

We have the calling and responsibility, as God's transforming agents in the world, to educate and train others according to God's purposes and desires. Education can bring transformation in people. We must raise up workers for God's Kingdom to become agents of the Syntropy Drama of God through education founded upon a Biblical worldview. Such a mission should be pursued not only by Handong Global University, but also by all other Christian universities. Such a mission is both a responsibility and a privilege for each one of us.

" This book is about an amazingly restorative
and redemptive work of God.
The Syntropy Drama of God unfolds
as His Word goes directly against the currents
of the world and brings about stunning
transformation to this universe. "

The Law of Syntropy I

Faith, the Assurance of Things Not Seen

Chapter 1

Calling and Obedience
At the Crossroads of My Life

From an Atheist Scientist
to a Creation Scientist

I was born into a typical Confucian family in the traditional town of Andong, Korea. Andong is located at the southeastern region of Korea, one of the most traditional and conservative regions of Korea. The city became famous worldwide when Queen Elizabeth of the United Kingdom visited it in April 1999. My family traces back our roots to the fourth son of the last King of the Shilla Dynasty (BC57-AD935); I am the 34th generation. I grew up instilled with the Confucian teaching "Kyoung-Chun-Ae-In" (written in Chinese as "敬天愛人"). It means "respect heaven, love people." Yet, I did not have a good grasp of the concept of "heaven."

After graduating from the College of Engineering at Seoul National University with a Bachelor of Science degree in metallurgical engineering and I continued my studies in the University of Missouri–Rolla with a Master of Science degree in metallurgical engineering. I then enrolled in the Ph.D. program in material science and engineering at Rensselaer Polytechnic Institute, in Troy, New York. Founded in 1824, Rensselaer is America's oldest technological university. While I was studying for my doctorate, my parents introduced me to a potential bride in Korea. In those days, such an introduction was very common. The woman, whom I had never met, was preparing to leave to study in the United States. With the encouragement of my parents, I began to court this young lady via letters. Although it may be difficult to imagine today, I proposed to her after we had gotten to know each other through the exchange of many letters.

The woman replied in response to my marriage

proposal. Her letter spelled out her precondition of marriage to me. She explained she was a Christian and she required me to believe in God and attend church with her if she was to marry me. The reality was that I had never attended church and there was not one person in my family who believed in Jesus Christ.

I responded by saying that, even though I had never thought about God or attended church, I would be willing to explore those things if there was a true "god" who would protect our family. I did not know what else to say, so I gave her a vague and dubious answer.

In reality, I was an atheist scientist and never believed that God had anything to do with science. I thought that it was inappropriate for a scientist to believe in the idea of a "spirit" or a spiritual world beyond the material world. A spiritual world to me was merely a product of the human imagination. But I did make the promise to her and after we got married, I had to keep that promise.

After getting married, we made our home together in the United States. As I flipped through the pages of the phone book to find the closest church, I asked my wife, "Which church did you attend: Presbyterian, Methodist, or Baptist?"

"Presbyterian," she replied.

The following day, we visited a white Presbyterian church near our home. It was my very first visit to any church. Not realizing what I was getting into, we sat in the front row only because I had a habit of sitting in the front row at every lecture in school. Not only that, but I had to listen quite attentively to the preacher in order to explain the content of the sermon to my wife, who was not quite fluent in English. The more I attended church, the more questions came to my mind. Nonetheless, I faithfully attended church every Sunday, just as I promised my wife.

Among the numerous incredible stories in the Bible, the one story in particular I simply could not accept was the supernatural conception of Jesus by the Virgin Mary. Whenever I asked my wife about it, her usual response was, "Don't question so much, and just believe the Bible!" There were clear differences between us. It seemed as if my wife was born with a set of DNA that permitted her to unconditionally believe in God. I was not like that. Despite my unbelief of Bible stories, I did conclude that Christian morality exceeded that of Confucianism.

> "But I tell you: love your enemies and pray for those who persecute you." (Matthew 5:44)

I had never heard anyone talk about loving our enemies, not even in the Confucian teaching of "Sam-Gang-Oh-Ryun," which means the teaching of "three bonds, five relationships." I thought to myself that I had nothing to lose by following Christianity, at least while living in the United States, especially since I felt that Christian morality presented a higher moral standard than Confucianism.

It was not until after I began working at NASA's Lewis Research Center in Cleveland, Ohio, following the completion of my Ph. D. degree that a new chapter in my life as a Christian finally opened up.

Believe This Illogical Bible?

NASA was a place I had dreamed of since my childhood. As a child, I was introduced to airplanes before automobiles and began to dream of the day I would build an airplane. My father started a temporary elementary school in the remote mountain village near Andong so that his eight children and other children in the village could study. He spent his entire life as the principal of the elementary school.

From time to time, my father brought home umbrellas made out of bamboo after attending meetings with other principals in the Andong area. I ripped the

Experimenting with high-temperature aerospace alloys at NASA in 1974

umbrellas apart to sort the bamboo sticks and turned them into airplane wing frames. I also used other types of wood and turned them into airplane propellers for my model plane. In an effort to produce a perfectly twisted propeller from wood, I would often accidentally cut myself with a sharp knife, leaving scars that are still visible today. I was truly passionate about building airplanes.

It turned out that my NASA days were more than a realization of my childhood dreams. Within NASA there was a small group prayer meeting that was held during lunch time every Tuesday. I was invited to this meeting by a devoted Christian colleague, Joe Mills. It was quite shocking to discover that preeminent scientists came together to study the Bible, to worship God and to pray. I immediately felt embarrassed about my thinking that having faith was a foolish idea.

After five years of being a churchgoer simply to satisfy my wife, I finally felt compelled to learn more about God and started to read the Bible. Based on recommendations, I began to read the Gospel of John.

As I read, I confronted an immediate obstacle to my faith. I read the record of the first miracle performed by Jesus Christ at the wedding at Cana in Galilee where He and His disciples were attending. When the wine ran out, Jesus Christ, when asked by Mary, His mother, commanded the servants to fill the jars with water and take the water to the master of the banquet. The Bible records that the servants obeyed Christ's seemingly ridiculous command and the water turned into wine (John 2:9). Somehow, the water molecular structure (H_2O) changed to a wine molecular structure (C_2H_5OH) in the course of delivery. Was I to believe this as a miracle? As a scientist, I could not accept this story as a fact for I knew that changes to molecular structures could not take place at ambient temperature under the conditions described in the story.

I asked my wife how anyone could believe such nonsense. My wife's response was always simple. She told me to believe without raising any questions. She even prodded me to believe saying that God would be offended by my doubts and questions. Despite the mounting doubts, I was determined to finish reading the Bible cover to cover and decided to temporarily put aside my doubts. As I resumed the reading, I encountered another stumbling block in John Chapter 6.

This was a story of how Jesus fed 5,000 people with five loaves of bread and two fish. A large crowd had been following Jesus on the hills across from the Sea of Tiberius of Galilee. Jesus saw that they were hungry and commanded His disciples to have them sit. Then Jesus took five loaves of bread and two small fish from a boy, gave thanks and distributed them among the crowd. The Bible records that after everyone had eaten their fill, the disciples gathered 12 baskets full of bread and fish that had been left over.

This story was even less believable than the water-turned-into-wine story. It defied the fundamental laws of science, in particular the Law of Conservation of Mass and Energy and the First Law of Thermodynamics. I concluded that the Bible was filled with too many illogical contradictions. My doubts continued to increase. I had to tell my wife that I would attend church because of my promise to her, but that I could not believe the Bible. As a legitimate scientist, I had to confront the fundamental question of "How can I believe in an invisible God?"

I started to feel that studying the Bible was a waste

of time and stopped reading the Bible altogether. I thought that I was better off in using my time for more productive research. Even when I changed my thinking, however, I had no peace in my heart.

As I was going through a phase of doubts and struggles regarding even the very existence of God, my Christian colleagues at NASA and certain members of Cleveland Korean Presbyterian Church told me that they were praying for me. Some of them were even fasting and praying at early morning prayer services for my faith. I could not believe that there were people who were skipping meals because of me. Because I did not want to be a burden to others, I decided to go back to the Bible reading again.

This time I started with Genesis, and looked for prophecies about the birth, life, death and the resurrection of Jesus Christ. (The Bible is a historical account with a single theme of God's redemption plan through Jesus Christ and written by about 40 authors over a period of about 1,600 years from different locations and perspectives.) I identified hundreds of prophecies about Jesus Christ from the Bible. The probability of fulfilling these prophecies by mere chance was mathematically impossible. Science is built on human knowledge and logic and is incapable of certainty as to what can take place even a second later. I began to affirm the Bible as historically reliable and absolutely credible when all the Old Testament prophecies written during a span of about 1,100 years were fulfilled in the New Testament. More importantly, my knowledge of the Bible began to prove to me that the Bible had to be given by God's inspiration, not by human knowledge or wisdom.

My earnest meditation on the Bible and research on scientific knowledge led me to the conclusion that there had to be a Creator God. This led to a trust in His sovereign power over human life. I finally took the very first step of Christian faith as I committed to believe in the Almighty Creator God through Jesus Christ.

I admit, however, far from being rock solid in my

faith, I continually oscillated between belief and un-belief. Just as a pendulum swings back and forth, I was tossed to and fro because of the fragility of my mind and the unfriendly environment.

My New Journey

Shortly before Easter 1974, I bought a book titled, *The Liberation of the Planet Earth* written by Hal Lindsey.[10]

This book gave explicit answers to many unre-solved questions for me. Who is God? Why was the Son of God born of the Virgin Mary? What is human sin? Why is the death of Jesus Christ the only solution to receive forgiveness of our sins? I was so interested in discovering the answers to these questions that I even skipped meals. I could not put the book down until well into the night. When I finished reading, I began to see the spiritual world opening up before me.

It was as if something like scales that had covered my eyes before was now finally falling off. My heart was filled with an indescribable joy. I experienced the understanding of truth which did not come through my knowledge but by the grace of God. It was the beginning of a new day and a new journey.

For the first time in my life, I began to understand certain attributes and characteristics of God: He is the Creator God who created all things in heaven and on earth, visible and invisible (Colossians 1:16). He is eternal, holy, omniscient, omnipotent and omnipresent. Also, He is the God of justice and love!

In the past, I could not understand why God would give freedom to the first man, Adam, to eat from all the trees of the Garden of Eden but would also commanded him to never eat from the tree of the knowledge of good and evil.

"And the LORD God commanded the man, 'You are free to eat from any tree in the garden; but you must not eat from the tree of the knowledge of good and evil, for when you eat from it you will certainly die.'"

(Genesis 2:16-17)

God did not create human beings as robots without personality. He gave man a free will to choose to obey His commands with a willing heart. By prohibiting man from eating from the tree of good and evil, God gave man a god-like ability to make choices. In so doing, God elevated man to personhood, like God Himself. The fruit from the tree of good and evil was a test God administered to man to determine whether man would obey or disobey the Word of God. However, Adam and Eve chose to eat the fruit from the tree of the knowledge of good and evil and just as God had declared, man became subject to spiritual and physical deaths.

"The Spirit gives life; the flesh counts for nothing."

(John 6:63)

"Our days may come to seventy years, or eighty, if our strength endures; yet the best of them are but trouble and sorrow, for they quickly pass, and we fly away." (Psalms 90:10)

Spiritual death means man's separation from God. Man listened to the voice of the Devil and became Satan's servant instead of remaining in God. However, God, out of His love, pursued mankind in order to save us from eternal punishment and to restore us as His children.

Life is in the blood (Leviticus 17:11), and without the shedding of blood there is no forgiveness (Hebrews 9:22). Accordingly, God provided a way of atonement through the shedding of the blood of unblemished animals. But an animal sacrifice could never be the perfect sacrifice of atonement.

"He did not enter by means of the blood of goats and calves; but he entered the Most Holy Place once for all by his own blood, thus obtaining eternal redemption." (Hebrews 9:12)

What was required to redeem sinful man was not an imperfect animal sacrifice but a perfect sacrifice, the person of Jesus Christ Himself. No other man could accomplish what Jesus could. In order to satisfy the requirements of atonement and redemption, the Son of God, conceived by the Holy Spirit, had to come in the form of man but without being touched by sin of any kind. In other words, God Himself had to come and die since there was no one else who qualified as a perfect sacrifice in order to pay the price of our sin.

"Look, the Lamb of God, who takes away the sin of the world!" (John 1:29)

"He is the atoning sacrifice for our sins, and not only for ours but also for the sins of the whole world."

(1 John 2:2)

"God presented Christ as a sacrifice of atonement, through the shedding of his blood—to be received by faith. He did this to demonstrate his righteousness, because in his forbearance he had left the sins committed beforehand unpunished." (Romans 3:25)

Jesus declared on the cross "It is finished" or "Tetelestai" in Greek. In a transactional context, it means "paid in full." When buying a house, one makes the initial down payment with the ultimate aim to make the final payment. When it is "paid in full," the title to the house is conveyed over to the buyer. At that point, the house belongs to the buyer. Similarly, we become God's possession when Jesus Christ paid the price in full.

Therefore, when we trust in the name of Jesus Christ and receive Him as our Savior and Lord, we receive a transformed identity as God's children belonging to Him alone.

> "For God so loved the world that he gave his one and only Son, that whoever believes in him shall not perish but have eternal life." (John 3:16)

John 3:16 explains the motivation, the price, the method and the goal of God's salvation plan of man. God's singular motivation was His love for us. God's price was the death of His one and only begotten Son, Jesus Christ. God's method was to save by man's faith in Jesus. God's goal was to give eternal life to man. It states the very essence of the Gospel of Jesus Christ. It also illustrates the magnificence of the grace of the Son of God.

As the Word of God flooded into my life, I began to understand the Bible. Until then, my knowledge of the Bible was at best fragmented. Once I began to understand the essence of the Gospel and the grace of Jesus Christ, all the pieces of the puzzle came together to form a clear picture that I would cherish the rest of my life.

In the process, I gained a clear understanding that the death of Jesus Christ on the cross 2,000 years ago was for my sins, and through believing in Him, I became a child of God. At last, after a long period of spiritual wandering, I finally received Jesus Christ, who is God and man, as my personal Savior and Lord.

"Yet to all who did receive him, to those who believed in his name, he gave the right to become children of God." (John 1:12)

My heart burned with excitement!

Filled with emotion, I turned to my wife and declared, "I finally know who God the Creator is, why He had to come down to this world in the flesh, and why He had to die on the cross." It was a shout of joy and great delight. As we held our hands and prayed, tears flowed down my cheeks.

"Oh Lord, why was I so blind to the truth of this Gospel until now? I am so sorry that I spent all these years in ignorance of the truth. Thank You for revealing the wonderful secrets of the Gospel tonight. How should we live in response to the grace we have received and to satisfy you?"

> "But God demonstrates his own love for us in this: While we were still sinners, Christ died for us." (Romans 5:8)

From a Spiritual Infant to a Proclaimer of the Gospel

The next morning, everything seemed different from the previous day. Even the fresh air blowing through the window, the trees in the garden, and the clear blue sky seemed different. I was filled with a joy that I had not felt before. I could finally understand the joy of my Christian NASA colleagues. It was a refreshing day overflowing with joy.

As I shared my testimony of how I received Jesus Christ to my NASA colleagues who had been praying for me, I broke into the hymn, "Amazing Grace."

Amazing grace, how sweet the sound,
  That saved a wretch like me.
  I once was lost but now am found,
  Was blind, but now I see.

T'was grace that taught my heart to fear.
  And grace, my fears relieved.
  How precious did that grace appear
  The hour I first believed.

Unbeknownst to me, God was writing His Syntropy Drama in our marriage and family. Since we were married after being introduced to each other by our parents, my wife and I discovered that we had very different personalities. Unlike my wife who is emotional, passionate and loves music and art, I was a typical Andong male: a man of few words who preferred to read books rather than engage in a conversation with my wife when I came home. So, you can imagine the kind of relationship we had. However, following my encounter with my Lord Jesus Christ, our dry and boring relationship became a more fun and exciting relationship. I like to compare the difference to drinking tap water versus sipping on a choice wine. We had a lot to talk about. We now shared the same worldview on the most important aspect our life together. Our Lord Jesus Christ was always at the center of our conversation.

I had to admit to my wife, "I feel remorse for thinking that Christianity was just another religion." The world considers Christianity to be one of many religions such as Confucianism, Buddhism, and Islam. They argue all religions are the same and their own religion is as good as Christianity. Now that I had personally encountered God, I knew such an argument could not be more wrong. My faith in God through Jesus Christ caused me to see things differently. I knew instantly that there had to be only one true God. I also knew that it was totally appropriate for me, as a creature, to worship the only true God who is the Creator.

> "'To whom will you compare me? Or who is my equal?' says the Holy One." (Isaiah 40:25)

In response to my confession and expression of faith in God, my wife said, "Your sermons are the best!" It was something very special for me to have been affirmed by my wife who had been a devoted Christian since her childhood. What's more, we truly became "one" in Christ at last. In spiritual reality, our new life together in Jesus meant that we began a "new marriage" in a fresh new way.

Encountering the People of God

A year later in June of 1975, the late Pastor Ja-Sil Choi who was widely known as the "Hallelujah Lady" came to speak at the Cleveland Korean Church revival meeting. She preached about the baptism of the Holy Spirit. The theme was "Did you receive the Holy Spirit when you first believed?"

> "Suddenly a sound like the blowing of a violent wind came from heaven and filled the whole house where they were sitting." (Acts 2:2)

> "On hearing this, they were baptized in the name of the Lord Jesus.
> When Paul placed his hands on them, the Holy Spirit came on them, and they spoke in tongues and prophesied." (Acts 19:5-6)

After the message, Pastor Choi invited us to a time

of "Tong-Sung-Gih-Do" (the style of prayer that made the Korean church famous and requires all of the congregants to pray out loud at the same time) in repentance. I had always thought that the baptism of the Holy Spirit was for those with a higher level of faith and I did not fit the bill. Pastor Choi laid her hands on the congregants and prayed for them. The entire sanctuary was filled with passionate prayer of repentance. Reflecting upon my life up to that point, I also offered up to God an earnest prayer of repentance. Suddenly, I experienced an indescribably strong presence of the Holy Spirit. I felt an irresistible power covering me and I wept uncontrollably.

God was changing me. God's grace was so refreshing every day. Tears of thankfulness always accompanied my singing of hymns, reading of the Bible or praying to God. God also changed me in other ways. God caused me to give up all alcoholic beverages. I was a long time drinker, a habit acquired from my father the art of drinking. Our home bar was replete with western style hard liquor and wines. I thought to myself, "Even Jesus turned water into wine" and had justified my drinking. One day, my wife and I were listening to an old sermon tape of the late Pastor Kyung-Chik Han who spoke on Ephesians 5:18, which read: "Do not get drunk on wine, which leads to debauchery. Instead, be filled with the Spirit."

Pastor Han preached: "We are the people running a race towards a finish line. Nobody runs a race with thick outerwear or in high heels. The runners necessarily must remove all things that would clutter and put on something light. The unedifying habits of this world are much like the heavy sandbags tied to the ankles of the runner. In order to complete the race, we must throw away the burdensome habits of this world."

It was no secret that drinking and smoking habits were unhealthy and harmful to our bodies. It was not very difficult for me to realize that my drinking and smoking habits had to stop if I was going to get rid of the hindrances in my race as a Christian. The message pierced my heart and I could not ignore the prompting of the Holy Spirit. I immediately took more than 30 bottles of hard liquor displayed at our home bar and emptied the bottles down the drain. As I eliminated alcohol from my life, my heart overflowed with living water.

"Therefore, if anyone is in Christ, the new creation has come: The old has gone, the new is here!" (2 Corinthians 5:17)

Changes in my life continued. My perspectives also underwent dramatic changes. Instead of insisting on humanistic knowledge-based perspectives, I embraced God-centered perspectives. Each day was filled with experiences of the grace of God and thankfulness to Him. In the midst of such blessings, God also blessed me academically. To my surprise, NASA acknowledged my research and achievements in the development of special high temperature alloy of aerospace applications, and presented me with my first NASA Tech Brief Award in 1974. All I could think was that to receive such an award within that highly academic setting was truly a work of God.

> "'Because he loves me,' says the LORD, 'I will rescue him; I will protect him, for he acknowledges my name.'" (Psalms 91:14)

Sometime later, God led me to a different job. Work at NASA required heavy concentration in research, which is what I desired, but I also wanted to be able to work where my research could be turned into practical applications. So, I looked for and found such a place. INCO (International Nickel Company) R&D Center in Suffern, New York. It was the world's largest nickel alloy-producing company and could satisfy both of my desires. INCO R&D Center conducted research on a specially developed nickel alloy that was used in aircraft and spacecraft engines.

One day, Dr. Raymond Decker, the technical vice president of INCO in New York visited NASA. I expressed my desire to work at INCO R&D Center and presented my work to him. In the middle of my presentation, he suddenly asked a strange question.

"Dr. Kim, I am already well aware of your research. I am more curious about your religion."

"I am a Christian," I replied.

Dr. Decker said, "I am a Christian, too. I am a Sunday Bible School teacher at my church in New York. Next week I have to teach about the Trinity. Could you help me with any ideas on how the Trinity could be explained?"

At that moment, I recalled something I had heard from Jong-Kyu Woo, M.D., who had a significant influence on my faith.

"It is probably inappropriate to illustrate the attributes of the triune of God, who is infinite in terms of finite things, but I have found it somewhat helpful to compare to the different properties of water," I said and continued, "Water's molecular structure is H_2O, but when it freezes it becomes solid ice. In room temperature, it turns into liquid water and when it evaporates, it becomes a gas or vapor. Could that possibly in some way illustrate how the triune God is one God with different functions?"

Dr. Decker nodded his head.

Soon after, I was recruited as an INCO R&D Center researcher. I could not tell you if that particular conversation had any impact upon Dr. Decker's decision to hire me. It is interesting, however, that such a conversation took place in my journey as a Christian.

My NASA Christian colleagues were very sad that I took a new position with INCO R&D Center, but they prepared a lovely farewell party for me. I appreciated their loving and sincere prayer for myself and my family.

"If INCO R&D Center does not have any Bible

study or a prayer meeting, we pray that you, Dr. Kim, should start one." they suggested.

Not long before I had been working at INCO R&D Center for a few days when Tilly Oaths, the secretary of the director of INCO R&D Center, came and asked me,

"Dr. Kim, you are always smiling and seem to be happy, what is your secret?"

"I gained a valuable research experience at NASA, and now I am working at INCO R&D Center, which is a job I've been desiring. Why shouldn't I be happy?" I responded.

"Is that all?" she asked.

Immediately, I realized I had left out an important secret.

I said, "In fact, the reason that I am happy is because I serve Jesus Christ as my Lord and Savior."

I could see her eyes sparkle. It turns out she was also a faithful Christian. She said joyfully,

"I have been praying for the past 20 years that we

would have a Bible study and prayer group at INCO R&D Center. Dr. Kim, let's start one, even though it might be just two of us. It will actually be three people because Jesus said that where two or three gather in His name there He is with them."

"For where two or three gather in my name, there am I with them." (Matthew 18:20)

The next day, we posted a new announcement on the bulletin board that read as follows:

Bible Study Every Wednesday at 12:30 p.m.
Attendees: Jesus, Young-Gil Kim, and Tilly Oaths

Twenty people came to the first meeting. It was as if everyone had been waiting for someone to initiate it. The Bible study at INCO R&D Center really taught me how to treasure Jesus in my life.

Sometime in 1978, my wife suggested that we should return to Korea permanently in order to lead my parents to Christ. Her challenge seemed quite unrealistic and unreasonable. After all, I was well into my fifth year at INCO R&D Center and was quite comfortable and content with my work. I was working in an ideal environment and was actively conducting wonderful research projects. All I could think was that I would like to stay at INCO R&D Center a few more years and gain more experience. Strangely, the burden of my wife's challenge did not subside with time. I started praying and asking God what I should do.

Around that time, I had an opportunity to attend a revival meeting at a New York Korean church where the late Pastor Chun-Seok Lee came and spoke.

"God, we are still spiritually young and cannot discern Your will. Please teach us Your will through Your servant," my wife and I prayed desperately.

On the last day of the meeting, Pastor Lee prayed

for us:

"My beloved son, go. Go without hesitation. I have prepared the way for you. Your hesitation is not my will. I will accomplish great things through you which others will not be able to do. In season and out of season, you must proclaim the Gospel. I will lead many people back to Myself through you."

We, and others who were praying with us, were all shocked to hear such a prayer. How could he pray a prayer like that when he had not known about our circumstances and when we had never met before?

"Surely the Sovereign LORD does nothing without revealing his plan to his servants the prophets." (Amos 3:7)

It was so very strange. Pastor Lee did not know the full meaning of his own prayer for he asked us, "Are you planning on leaving the United States?"

"These are the things God has revealed to us by his Spirit. The Spirit searches all things, even the deep things of God." (1 Corinthians 2:10)

How wondrous that the Holy Spirit pays attention to our personal needs and circumstances! Through Pastor Lee's amazing prayer, we came to realize that God had planned for us to return to Korea. God had in mind for us a new beginning and all of this was a demonstration of His providential calling in my life.

Shortly thereafter, I submitted my resignation to Dr. Howard Merrick, my supervisor. He was greatly surprised and strongly advised against it. He was convinced that my decision to return to Korea was because I was homesick and offered me a 6-month leave so that I could visit Korea and return to work. But, as I knew that God wanted me to return to Korea, Dr. Merrick could not change my mind.

In December of 1978, after having lived in the United States for twelve years, my wife and I returned to Korea with two of our children. I took a position as an overseas-invited professor of Material Engineering at KAIST.

Syntropy Drama Unfolded in My Family

As soon as we returned to Korea, we went to visit my elderly mother in my hometown of Andong for we had not seen her in almost ten years. I stayed with her and shared the Gospel.[11]

"The Bible says we are all sinners. What do you think about this?" I asked my mother.

My mother had an interesting response: "Of course, humans are all sinners. Humans are evil! We pull and eat all the vegetables from the soil, we eat all the fish in the oceans, eat all the birds that fly, and all the words that we say are either evil or lies. So definitely we are sinners! It's scarier to meet a person in the street at night than to come across a wild animal.

And, of course, I am a sinner, too. Yes, I have sinned a lot."

To my surprise, she had no trouble acknowledging and accepting that she was a sinner. And that very night she accepted Jesus in her heart as I led her in praying the sinner's prayer.

> "For it is with your heart that you believe and are justified, and it is with your mouth that you confess and are saved." (Romans 10:10)

Although she prayed the sinner's prayer with me, she apparently continued to have lingering doubts in her mind. One day, my late older brother, Dr. Ho-Gil Kim, the former founding president of POSTECH (Pohang University of Science and Technology) came to see our mother. So she asked him a question:

"My son, do you think the Dragon King is higher, or is Jesus higher?"

My brother laughed out loud for some time and answered, "Mother, just think of Jesus as your big brother and the Dragon King as your little brother. And if we are going to believe in anyone, we should believe in the big brother." My brother's comic answer seemed to soothe her concern and she said, "Son, do you think so too? Thanks for letting me know."

A few days later my mother came to visit us in Seoul and there she was baptized. As she was quite old, she could not attend church, but she read the Bible as best she could and prayed every day. She knew enough to boldly throw away the jar in which she kept her household god. Every day she slowly recited the Lord's Prayer and Apostle's Creed as she was praying.

In October 1986, about seven years after my mother received Christ, my father came home from having attended the closing ceremony of the Asian Games. He seemed deeply troubled. It was written all over his face, but he did not say anything right away. After a few days, he began to tell us what happened inside the taxi cab on his way to the closing ceremony.

The taxi cab driver had asked my father, "So you came all the way from Andong to see the closing ceremony. You seem very happy today."

"Yes, everyone says that I'm a blessed man and is quite envious of me," my father proudly told him.

Out of nowhere, the taxi cab driver asked, "But sir, do you believe in Jesus?"

To this my father gave a rather interesting answer, "I don't, but my fourth son (that's me), his wife, his son and his daughter do believe in Jesus."

The taxi cab driver brilliantly responded to my father, "Sir, you know that you cannot enter the stadium if you don't have your own ticket, right? Likewise, it doesn't matter even if your family members believe in Jesus. You have to believe. And, unless you yourself believe in Jesus, your name is not registered in the Book of Life. Sir, since you are already up in age, why not receive Jesus and be prepared for heaven?"

My wife and I knew, right there and then, that we

could not waste this wonderful opportunity! We mustered all our courage and began to tell my father about Jesus. Coming from a very Confucian background, it was not an easy task for a son to tell his father that he is a sinner. You see, my father was highly regarded by others and was a man of tremendous morality and character. It would be completely against Confucian teaching for a son to tell his father how sinful he was. But that is exactly what I did.

My father was clearly bothered by it and said, "Whenever I come to your home, your kids are always talking about this Jesus. Oh my, so you and your household, right down to your kids are all infected with this Jesus thing. I am not sure about this."

But, God was already working in my father's heart. Before the night was over, my father prayed to receive Jesus into his heart with me. My father prayed, "Lord God, I have not realized until this day that not knowing you is a sin. So I receive you into my heart as my Savior and Lord. Please be my guide until I go to heaven."

A few months later, when my father was also baptized, he said to the late Rev. Yong-Jo Hah, who administered the baptism, "I am told that everyone must receive Jesus personally to get the ticket to heaven. That is why I am here."

My father had stepped inside of a church for the first time in his life. One Friday afternoon, in a nearly empty sanctuary, my father was baptized in the presence of several pastors. As we witnessed my father being baptized on his knees, we all wept out of joy.

"Salvation is found in no one else, for there is no other name under heaven given to men

by which we must be saved." (Acts 4:12)

After this, most of our family members who used to be proud of following Confucianism and being members of the "yangban" class (the class known as the aristocrats during the Chosun Dynasty in Korea and steeped in tradition) came to receive Jesus.

"Believe in the Lord Jesus, and you will be saved—
you and your household." (Acts 16:31)

From Evolutionist
to Creationist

Once I returned to Korea, my family was provided
with a condominium within the National Science Park
located at Hongreung in Seoul. This was the official
housing provided for the scientists and faculty members of the Korea Institute of Science and Technology
(KIST) and KAIST, where I worked. The science complex was built by the late Korean President Jung-Hee
Park as an incentive to attract and recruit outstanding
scientists and researchers who could help develop Korea's economic growth.

The Science Village was no ordinary place. It was

known as the Mecca of Korean science. Yet, God would work mysteriously within the Village in such a way that out of such a place where science had become everyone's idol, the Christian scientists within the Village would grasp the fallacies of the theory of evolution and spawn the creation science movement in Korea. God does indeed work in ways that are beyond human experiences.

In retrospect, it was no accident that the Korean Association for Creation Research (KACR) was founded within the Science Village in Seoul, Korea. God chose the KIST and KAIST Science Village to do His work. There were about 400 scientists living in the Science Village in 1978. We formed a Bible study for Christian scientists. It was led by Pastor Yong-Jo Hah (then the founding pastor of the Entertainer's Church that was largely composed of scientists, singers, movie stars and entertainers, etc.) and most of the founding members of KACR lived in the Science Village. God had arranged all this.

In August 1980, an international conference entitled "The Origin of Life: Evolution or Creation?" was held in Seoul during the 1980 World Evangelical Congress. An international panel of speakers such as Dr. Henri Morris who was the founding president of the Institute of Creation Research (ICR), Dr. Duane Gish, Dr. Bradley and others from the United States were slated to speak. But the Korean panel was not yet been finalized.

As Rev. Joon-Gon Kim, the founder of Korean Campus Crusade for Christ (KCCC) was looking for a Korean speaker for the conference, I was visited by Yong-Gee, a KCCC member. He said, "Dr. Kim, we desperately need a Korean speaker at the conference. Apparently, no biologists are willing to be the speaker for creation science. I believe it is because no one wants to become an outcast in the academic community by officially taking sides with creation science and rejecting the theory of evolution. So will you please be the Korean speaker?"

My response was, "I don't think I'm qualified because my expertise is not in life science but in materials science and engineering."

But Dr. Shim would not take "No" for an answer. In fact, he visited me almost every day although I rejected his request every time. I could no longer refuse and finally relented, "Fine! Since no one is willing to do it, I will regard it as God's command and do it. But please bring me materials related to creation science."

Dr. Shim then brought me about ten books on creation science and evolution. By that time, there were only two weeks remaining before the conference. I had never studied harder before than during the following two weeks.

I already believed in Genesis 1:1 that God created the universe, but I was not prepared to scientifically argue against the theory of evolution. After studying the books that Dr. Shim had brought, however, I was able to gain a level of confidence about the theories of the origin of life.

"For since the creation of the world God's invisible qualities—his eternal power and divine nature—have been clearly seen, being understood from what has been made, so that men are without excuse." (Romans 1:20)

Creationism or Evolution?

Though I did not have much time to prepare for the international conference, God gave me confidence and understanding so that I could prepare for the presentation with conviction in my heart. At the conference, I boldly presented the scientific evidences of creationism as well as inconsistencies with the evolution theory. The following is an excerpt from my first talk on creation science at the international creation science conference.

There are two models on the origin of life; evolution and creation. The evolution model is a naturalistic, mechanistic process and it excludes the act of God. The creation model states that God created life with His intelligence and design, and every living thing was brought into existence by acts of God. It depends on the Creator's intelligence, while the evolution model depends on time and chance.[12]

• Life comes only from existing living life:

The greatest biologist of the 19th century was Louis Pasteur of France (1822-1895). He conducted an experiment which rejected the theory of the spontaneous generation of life. He demonstrated that life comes only from pre-existing life. If life can only come from life, then where did the first life come from? This leads to a conclusion that God created the first form of life in the very beginning. As in Genesis 1, God created every living thing after its kind. Various life forms were created by God separately after their kinds.

• Fossil record supports creation model:

Fossils are hardened remains, or traces of life preserved in the earth's crust. Many people believe that fossils are substantial evidence for proof of evolution theory. If evolution is a fact, there would be more than 1.5 million transitional forms linking each species since there are about 1.5 million species living on the Earth. Therefore, one would expect numerous numbers of transitional forms of fossils. However, there are no fossils showing a gradual evolutionary progression throughout time. The fossil record gives excellent support for the creation model.

On November 3, 1980, the *Newsweek* magazine published an article on the topic of macro-evolution and micro-evolution. The article claimed that "In the fossil records, missing links are the rule." The article went on to say that the more scientists look for fossil evidence of macro-evolution, the more they become frustrated. Shortly prior to the *Newsweek* article in October 1980, a historic conference on "Evolutionary Theory Under Fire" was held in Chicago, challenging the four-decade long dominance of the modern synthesis. The conference concluded that micro-evolution cannot provide evidence for macro-evolution.[13] We have to distinguish between macro-evolution and micro-evolution. Micro-evolution is "sub-speciation," which is the variation within a species, while macro-evolution is "trans-speciation", which is the change from one type to others. It is true that the processes of mutation and natural selection produce micro-evolution (variation within type). But we have not observed the occurrence of macro-evolution. Macro-evolution requires the expansion of the gene pool and the addition of new genes to produce new species and new complex organs.

• Thermodynamic laws do not support evolution:

The two laws of thermodynamics are known to be the most basic and universal laws of science. The first law of thermodynamics known as the law of conservation of energy states that the total amount of energy in the universe remain unchanged. This means that energy can neither be created nor destroyed, but can only be transformed. If this is the case, then where did the initial energy come from? The logical answer is to say that it must have been created by God—from nothing to matter (energy).

The second law of thermodynamics also known as the law of increasing entropy states that as time elapses, everything runs down and tends towards the state of randomness, thus, the highest entropy. This contradicts the theory of chemical evolution which assumes that inorganic substances organize themselves to produce complex order of life forms. Even in an open system, a pre-existent mechanism is necessary for increasing the degree of order.

• Mathematical probability says "No" to evolution:

The logic of science is based on mathematics. What is the mathematical probability of forming a living cell purely by chance? The cell is the basic structure which makes up living things, and it is basically made up of protein and DNA. Suppose that there are 100 amino acids. What would be the probability of forming a specific sequence of 100 amino acids for a protein? The probability is 1 out of 10^{130} $(1/10^{130})$. This probability is essentially zero. Therefore, Dr. R. W. Kaplan states that life could not have originated without a donor of life.[14] In the creationist view, there is information in DNA and the formation of information demands intelligence. Therefore, DNA was formed by intelligence. DNA is somewhat like a computer program on a floppy disk. Like a computer disk, DNA, itself has no intelligence. The complex codes of DNA could only have originated outside of itself.

I presented the core distinction between life and lifelessness. Consider a dead seed and a live seed. Both seeds possess the same organic structure and composition. However, if the dead seed is buried underneath the soil, it will decay and rot. On the contrary, if the live seed is buried, it will produce little stems and leaves and grow into a plant that will flower and bear fruit. In the living seed, there is a mysterious source of invisible energy or power that the dead seed does not possess. Life is not merely material, but rides upon matter. Life can be defined by what it does, not by what it is. The invisible source of life is given by the invisible Creator God.

The Creationism Conference Caused a Great Stir

About 4,000 students, pastors, scientists and others attended the "Creation or Evolution" Conference for two days. By all accounts, the event was successful. But I was more impressed with the fact so many people came and showed their interest in the question of the origin of life. It really caught me by surprise.

I could sense a very passionate crowd. As I took the stage to speak, I felt the presence of God and was able to speak with power and wisdom. Quite unexpectedly, the conference on creation science stirred up not only Korean churches but also the rest of Korea as many of the major daily newspapers carried articles on creation science. Creation science was both revolutionary and sensational to many who had always thought that faith and science could not be combined.

Not all newspaper articles were favorable. One article expressed concerns for the future of science in Korea because the KIST and KAIST Science Village embraced certain unscientific scientists who could not distinguish religion from science. One science reporter actually called me by phone and viciously criticized me. Another article said that instead of focusing on the scientific research I was invited to carry on in Korea, I was engaging in religious activities by espousing the creation theory and criticizing evolution theory, which had been accepted as the standard of science.

As I was getting a beating from the secular press, God demonstrated His uncanny sense of timing and humor. What God did literally quenched the fiery attacks of the secular press who called me an "unscientific scientist." You see, I became a recipient of not one but two major awards given to scientists. And they both came years after I left NASA and INCO Research Center. One was the NASA Tech Brief Award. The other was the Industrial Research Award (IR-100). Both awards recognized the invention of a super heat-resistant alloy used in jet engines (MA-6000), which NASA and INCO Research Center developed jointly. God defended me when I could not defend myself. The press could no longer call me an "unscientific scientist." God's timing was perfect!

I believed that God blessed me as a Christian scientist so that I could diligently pursue creation science. For example, I was blessed to work jointly with Poongsan Corporation and under the auspices of the Ministry of Science and Technology of Korea. During this time I was able to invent and produce PMC-102, a special alloy used in a semi-conductor lead frame.

This alloy was patented in the United States, Japan, and Germany, and the technology was licensed to Stolburger, Inc. producing copper alloys in Germany. This was the first Korean technology export to a foreign country, for which I received a Dong-Baek-Jang, an "Order of Civil Merit" medal from the government.

God would continually bless me with the fruits of the research I was so privileged to be part of or lead. For example, I went on to invent CAM-1, an alloy of two seemingly incompatible qualities. This particular alloy, on the one hand was harder and, on the other hand, more ductile than other metals of its kind than in existence at cryogenic temperatures. For this invention, I received a prestigious King Sejong Cultural Award from the Korean government in the field of science. In 1987, I was chosen as the Scientist of the Year by science reporters for my invention of W-250, a super strong and tough tungsten alloy. It was God's way of restoring me as a legitimate scientist after the media heavily criticized me for my stance on creation science. At the same time, creation science took on more notoriety. Naturally, creation science became better known and the people began to give more respect to creation scientists and the work of the Korea Association for Creation Research (KACR).

"Surely you desire truth in the inner parts; you teach me wisdom in the inmost place." (Psalms 51:6)

I have no doubt in my mind that all my achievements were a direct result of God's blessing and wisdom. By demonstrating that one can be a true scientist and a creation scientist, God opened up the doors for me to more effectively share the Gospel.

"But seek first his kingdom and his righteousness, and all these things will be given to you as well." (Matthew 6:33)

The Syntropy Ministry of the Korean Association for Creation Research (KACR)

In January of 1981, the year following the CCC's creation science conference, about 20 Christian scientists formed KACR.

Rev. Joon-Gon Kim made the following remarks about KACR: "If I were to identify three critical events in Korean church history, they are: one, the arrival of the first official missionaries, Appenzeller and Underwood in 1885; two, the completion of the Korean Bible translation in 1911; and three, the birth of KACR that will challenge evolution theory in 1981."

The purpose of KACR was to spread the Gospel of Jesus Christ by showing the world dominated by evolution theory, a significant body of evidence that God created the heavens and the earth. As the founding president of KACR, my colleagues and I conducted seminars and offered lectures on creation science all around the country. All this was possible, not because of my knowledge or experience, but because the Holy Spirit residing in me strengthened me. Because I was so excited about the ministry that God had given me, my colleagues and I were neither tired nor weary even though we constantly traveled long distances. We were never bored even though we gave the same lectures over and over again. Every time I testified for the God of Creation, I experienced the grace and presence of God.

A Precious Gift

One day in 1987, a student that I met at the Chong-Shin Seminary's freshman orientation visited me and asked, "Dr. Kim, would you be willing to come and speak to my tiny countryside church on creation science?"

"Sure, I will go anywhere as long as I have time," I

said assuredly.

After a while, the invitation came. The church was located in the outskirts of the Paju village in the north of Seoul. Although Paju was not too far from Seoul, it was quite a challenge getting there. The trip took a long time and really tested my endurance as I had to travel over the unpaved winding countryside roads. Upon arrival, I noticed some traditional cottages in the village but the church was nowhere in sight. I was told that Paju was the birthplace of a noble named Lee , Hang-Bok during the Yi Dynasty. While wandering in the middle of the village, I noticed a small house with a cross on the top. There I was treated with a very simple but delicious meal prepared by that student's family.

With big smiles, the seminarian said, "Dr. Kim, I wasn't sure if you would really come to this tiny and shabby place to speak. Now, I'm only grateful that you came all the way out here."

"I was born and grew up in a village just like this

one. The dinner tasted even better because this place reminded me of my birthplace," I said in response.

The student then made a request, "Dr. Kim, after your lecture, an old grandmother asked to see you. Will you meet with her?"

After loading the slide projector, we moved into another room. It was just large enough for 20 people to sit, and it had a wood-burning stove. There were only five or six old grandmothers and a few elementary students. I knew that a full slide presentation would not be suitable and that I had to simplify my lecture. So I spoke briefly on creation science and shared my testimony about how I became a Christian.

After my testimony, an old grandmother held my hand and pulled out two 10,000 Korean Won bills (about US$2) from her inner pants' pocket.

The grandmother slowly opened her mouth and said, "Dr. Kim, I'm so grateful that you came all the way to this tiny village. I've prayed for tonight for many months and prepared this small token of appreciation. So you must take this."

I was very touched by the grandmother's gesture but I said, "Dear grandmother, God has blessed all the speakers at KACR with their own jobs and we always give lectures as volunteers. Your thoughts are more than enough and thank you."

It was useless to keep refusing her as she kept on insisting that I accept her gift. Although I have traveled and spoken in many places, the old grandmother's gift was the most touching and meaningful gift I had ever received.

After my experience in Paju, I had to share a compelling thought on my mind with KACR officers:

"I would like to propose that from now on, we should not be concerned with the numbers of attendees at our lectures. Even if a small number of people attend the lecture, there may be even one person likely to be saved. Could we be satisfied and grateful by the fact that we are used by God in this work? I believe God does not care as much about the numbers than about saving one lost soul."

It was as if God poured out His blessings upon KACR. Requests for lectures flooded in from many churches and mission agencies as well as from university festivals. Our creation science lectures challenged and shook up non-believers but bolstering the faith of Christians.

"I am the voice of one calling in the desert." (John 1:23)

John the Baptist was a "voice in the wilderness" that faithfully proclaimed the Creator God. I wondered if I too could be used as a voice in the science wilderness for God. So, whenever I delivered the lectures, I always did so passionately regardless of the size of the audience. I learned to not focus on the reactions of the audience but more on whether or not I was faithful in carrying out my duties as the voice of God. One might think that I would have been tired of repeating the same lectures again and again. Quite to the contrary, each and every time I was able to proclaim Jesus Christ as the Creator with passion, joy and assurance flooded my soul.

KACR achieved many milestones but there was one milestone we could not achieve. We came so close to winning the bid to include creation science in the middle and high-school textbooks. We felt that this would have been a very meaningful achievement, particularly because all the textbooks at that time only included evolution theory even though this is not a proven theory. By 1989, we were successful in passing the first two levels of evaluation but failed to pass the third-level evaluation. As a result, we were not successful in revising the textbooks to include creation science.

Though we could not revise the high school biology textbooks, we were able to modify the college textbooks because, unlike high-schools, universities are free to choose their own textbooks. We had to come up with college textbooks that included creation science theory so that anyone could objectively compare evolution and creation science theories. The founder of Myongji University, Dr. Sang-Geun Yoo, supported us by saying, "If KACR can come up with a textbook that includes creation science theory, Myongji University will use it as liberal arts textbook." Finally, 20 professors of KACR from various majors completed the project. *Natural Science*, a textbook from KACR, was published in May 1990, and it covered 12 topics including material, earth, universe, origin of life, biotechnology, computer, energy, etc. It was first adopted at Myongji University and later used by various universities and seminaries. In Handong Global University, the Creation and Evolution Class is mandatory for all students since its inception in 1995.

The hymn "How Great Thou Art" is KACR's theme song. The lyrics of this hymn contain the entire Gospel. The first and second verses talk about God as the Creator, the third verse is about Jesus who died on the cross for our sins, and the last verse is about our personal encounter with Jesus. When we sing the last verse, I would lead people to Christ by inviting them to stand if they wanted to receive Jesus into their hearts.

Verse 1: O Lord my God, when I in awesome wonder, consider all the worlds thy hands have made; I see the stars, I hear the rolling thunder, thy power throughout the universe displayed.

Verse 2: When through the woods, and forest glades I wander, and hear the birds sing sweetly in the trees. When I look down, from lofty mountain grandeur and see the brook, and feel the gentle breeze.

Verse 3: And when I think, that God, His Son not sparing; sent Him to die, I scarce can take it in; that on the Cross, my burden gladly bearing,

He bled and died to take away my sin.

Verse 4: When Christ shall come, with shout of acclamation, and take me home, what joy shall fill my heart? Then I shall bow, in humble adoration, and then proclaim: "My God, how great Thou art!"

Chorus: Then sings my soul, my Savior God, to Thee, how great thou art, how great thou art. Then sings my soul, my Savior God, to Thee, how great thou art, how great thou art!

From Professor at KAIST
to President of Handong Global University

While I was a professor at KAIST in February of 1994, a friend of mine called me one day. He said a new Christian university was starting in Pohang, called Handong Global University, and they wanted to invite me as the first president. I politely declined the offer because for the past 25 years I had only taught with research and had no experience in university administration. However, the information that a Christian university would be founded on Christian faith always stuck on my mind.

Soon after I returned from America in 1979, I visited Jesus Abbey in Taebek, Gangwondo, to see Ruben Archer Torrey III (1918-2002) because I was reminded of what he shared with me. "Harvard and Yale University were first founded on pure Christian faith, but as time went by, their foundation got weak as they educated only academic knowledge. Therefore I've prayed for a long time that a Christian university with pure faith should be founded in Korea that integrates spirituality, knowledge, and character."

I did not regard this as my task because, back then, I was just returning to Korea as a professor at KAIST.

But, after receiving the invitation from Handong, I had a burden in my heart. My wife and I started to pray for discernment to see whether the call was from my friend or from God.

It was not easy to let go of a great research position and a guaranteed future at KAIST. Many of my colleagues also insisted that I stay, and my students in the Masters and Ph.D. programs were also discouraged upon hearing the news of the possibility of my departure. Even my elder brother who was the first founding president of POSTECH dissuaded me.

"You are in your glory days of research. Stopping that job at KAIST now and taking a new administration position in charge of a university will be a national loss."

Then he added one thought.

"But since Handong will be founded on Christian faith, if you are making your decision based on Christian faith, I would not be able to stop you. However, starting a new university that focusses on the whole person education, cultivating the 21st century's industrial elites toward global Christian leadership would also be a great contribution to our country."

A few days later, the founder of Handong asked me to visit the school. Before the visit, God spoke to my heart through many different channels. The week I was invited to visit Handong, the title of the Sunday sermon at my church was "Calling for Obedience." (Genesis 12:1-4)

My pastor's sermon began:

"God sometimes calls us out from our comfort zone in order to send us to the suffering parts of creation. The first reason is to learn to truly rely upon God. It is not easy to learn to rely upon God when we are comfortable. The second reason is to learn to be free. We cannot experience true freedom from where we are now because of our position, honor, name, and pride. But those who obey and leave because of God's calling must learn how to let go of all worldly things. Though there will be much sufferings, we can be truly free. God promised this to those that obey Him."

> "I will make you into a great nation and I will bless
> you; I will make your name great, and you will be a
> blessing. I will bless those who bless you, and who-
> ever curses you I will curse; and all peoples on earth
> will be blessed through you." (Genesis 12:2-3)

Our pastor's sermon was like God speaking to us through a loudspeaker. As we listened to the sermon, my wife and I wept again and again as we wiped our tears and exchanged our handkerchiefs. At the end of the sermon, the pastor concluded by saying, "But there is one thing you must remember when you leave your comfort zone. You should not look at the condition or circumstances, but follow only the Word of God (Genesis 12:4). You might not have a bright future. Like Abraham, you might meet famine or unwanted hardships and persecutions."

By the end of the sermon, my wife and I prayed for

God's will to be done in our lives. And at last we decided that I would accept the position as the first president of Handong Global University.

God's Calling vs. Rational Decision

From that point, I started planning a roadmap to begin a university based on genuine Christian faith as I went to and from Seoul, between the KAIST Science Park and Pohang. I received much needed advice from my elder brother as I stayed most of my weekends at his home in Pohang. Then on April 30, 1994, one month after I accepted this position, I heard shocking news. My elder brother whom I truly loved and respected as a mentor passed away in an unexpected accident. Our whole family went into shock and was very deeply saddened. Soon after that, my parents passed away. In one year's time, my beloved family members passed away one by one. However, I did not have time to properly grieve the loss of my dear family members because I had to prepare the launch of a new university.

In June of the same year, I was visiting several cities in the United States to invite new professors. After visiting Los Angeles and San Francisco, I was in Boston when I received an urgent phone call from my wife. There was a story in the news that Handong's founder had to stop his business due to an unexpected industrial accident. I heard this news as I was making a presentation about Handong Global University to a group of people. I was standing at a crossroad. Should I continue to share about this new university, or should I not? I still do not know what came over me at the time, but I kept sharing my new educational vision for the 21st century as scheduled without any hesitation and with even more courage. When I returned to Korea, the school founder explained what the situation was.

"Because the financial hit is severe, it is impossible

to open the university next year as planned. But, Dr. Kim, if you can receive help from Korean churches, please continue what you have been working on. But if you want to return to KAIST, I'm willing to cancel everything."

My hesitancy was incomparable to the time when I first received the offer of presidency. Should I go on or stop? How could I explain God's calling that we accepted from our pastor's sermon a few months ago? Should I obey the call or stop continuing the work based on a rational decision? My wife and I knelt before the Lord every morning at the altar.

I had been proclaiming about God the Creator who created the universe out of nothing at numerous creation science seminars. How should I apply this notion in my life now? Was I trusting the Almighty God, the Creator of the universe? It is easy to say that I trust God when the circumstances are good. But continuing in the present situation simply seemed foolish. Nevertheless, would I not be limiting God's work in my life? I was totally lost. Was God leading me to a place I did not want to go in order to teach me a lesson on how to trust Him completely?

> "I tell you the truth, when you were younger you dressed yourself and went where you wanted; but when you are old you will stretch out your hands, and someone else will dress you and lead you where you do not want to go." (John 21:18)

Still, God created a number of circumstances such that I could not escape Handong Global University. The chairman of a Christian business group who was interested in establishing a university came and visited the school. We presented our plan to him, and he responded positively. We waited for his reply with anticipation. After four months of waiting, he replied that they could not take on the university. The school's opening was in its final stage and invitations to the professors had already been sent. The despair I felt was incomprehensible since some professors had already moved to Pohang by then. It was too late to stop the opening of the school. Rev. Yong-Jo Hah of Onnuri Church knew everything about our circumstances and prayed earnestly for us. Knowing of our desperate situation, Onnuri Church contributed 3 billion Korean Won (about US$3 million) which was needed to get the approval from the Ministry of Education. After many twists and turns, Handong Global University finally received approval from the government on December 2, 1994.

The school barely opened on March 7, 1995, without having solid financial support. Nonetheless, the school had a clear vision. We had a calling to go forth as a "new Christian university for the 21st century with a vision of a new education system that would be God's university". As a result, 4,872 students applied in the first year when we only had space for 400 students. It was an unprecedented event for a university in such a rural city, and this was covered as headline news. The admitted students' scores were comparative to those of leading universities' students in Korea.

God was calling forth obedience through adventure, so that Handong would take some of the responsibility for the demands of the 21st century global community.

"'Do I bring to the moment of birth and not give delivery?' says the LORD. 'Do I close up the womb when I bring to delivery?' says your God." (Isaiah 66:9)

Syntropy Drama Continued In Prison

"For you, O God, tested us; you refined us like silver. You brought us into prison and laid burdens on our backs. You let men ride over our heads; we went through fire and water, but you brought us to a place of abundance." (Psalms 66:10-12)

God's work cannot be accomplished without going through a test of fire. We, God's children, must go through the same test as Joseph, Daniel, Esther, Mordecai, Jeremiah, Paul, the Apostles and our ancestors of faith did. Although Handong finally opened after many difficulties, more problems ensued: ongoing extreme financial shortages, demands to shift our university to a city college by local leaders, and unproven accusations. As a result, many lawsuits flooded in. In addition to that, after the Asian economic crisis the IMF came in 1997 and we were not able to get loans even with high interest. All sorts of persecutions and countless trials were part of the tests of fire from God. But it is also God who controls the temperature of the fire. We had to completely trust God who was training us with the degree of the temperature just right for us.

"When you pass through the waters, I will be with you; and when you pass through the rivers, they will not sweep over you. When you walk through the fire, you will not be burned; the flames will not set you ablaze." (Isaiah 43:2)

Whenever a crisis arose, He led me to trust Him more than to trust men. Though the trials and pains were hard, in God I slowly realized that they were blessings in disguise. God sometimes provided me paths to avoid extreme crisis and sometimes provided finances in extreme difficulties by means of exquisite timing.

"It was good for me to be afflicted so that I might learn your decrees." (Psalms 119:71)

I often read and mediated on *Imitation of Christ* by Thomas a Kempis. One passage was particularly memorable: "There are many that love Jesus to gain salvation and go to heaven. But there are extremely few that are willing to bear Jesus' cross and suffering. There are many that are willing to enjoy the happiness and blessing in Jesus. But there are extremely few that are willing to participate in the sacrifice and pain with Jesus Christ."[15]

Prison No. 433

May 11, 2001, Pohang Courtroom:

"The defendant has intentionally avoided a court appearance without probable cause, and has frequently gone overseas for business trips without purpose. In addition, there is a risk for the defendant tampering with the evidence and a possibility of escaping Korea and heading overseas. Therefore, due to the nature of his crime, I order two years in prison for the defendant."

When the judge in the local court had finished reading the verdict and asked if I had anything to say, I was unable to answer. My mind was stupefied and I could not comprehend what the verdict meant: "embezzlement," "risk of tampering with the evidence," "intentional avoidance of court appearance without a probable cause," "a possibility of escaping Korea and heading overseas." Before I could think clearly, the correctional officers came in and took me through the court's back doors. Once we stepped out through the door, they put handcuffs on me. Reality finally hit me when I felt the cold handcuffs on my wrists.

I had been working so hard, frantically running back and forth raising funds for the construction fee of a new school dormitory and trying to pay the existing school debt. Just then, the Ministry of Education selected Handong's achievement of academic reform for the 21st century and the school received the total amount of US$1.3 million from the government. With that financial support, I first gave overdue salaries to our professors because I knew how much they had been suffering due to not getting paid on time. Soon thereafter, we were able to completely make up the total government supported fund with other financial resources that came in.

However, I was accused of misusing government funds. In addition, I was accused of violating the labor law for not paying the professors' salaries for three months. I was also sued for embezzlement for not paying the lawyer fee with my personal money. I was investigated and had to face numerous trials because of ongoing accusations and lawsuits. Finally, the vice president and I were sentenced to 18 months and 24 months each in May of 2001. This happened after about 40 investigations by the police and prosecutors. Putting the President and vice president under immediate court custody was an unprecedented event in the history of Korean universities.

While I was being led to Kyongju prison, I closed my eyes in the steel-barred bus. I began to wonder what the will of God might be through this unbelievable and helpless situation. The only thing that came to my mind was how much all my beloved family, students, professors, staff and students' parents could have been shocked. Thinking about their shock caused my heart to ache for them. I was at a complete loss. I did not know how to pray to God.

"And we know that in all things God works for the good of those who love him, who have been called according to his purpose." (Romans 8:28)

Students and parents at prison gate on Teacher's Day, May 15, 2001

At Kyongju Prison, I was taken with other prisoners into one room. The prisoners who were on trial were kept at the detention center, but prisoners who were not on trial were locked up in prison. The prisoners with confirmed sentences wore blue uniforms and prisoners who were waiting for trial wore brown uniforms. As directed by the prison officer, I took off all my clothes and put them in a sack, and picked up a brown uniform from a pile in a corner under their orders. But the pants that I had picked up were too big so I bent over to look for a smaller pair, but the guard said, "Just wear anything! They're all the same, no point in choosing." I took off my shoes and put on the white rubber shoes.

"Take off your glasses! Prison rules do not allow metal-framed glasses. Tell your family to bring you plastic-rimmed glasses when they visit you."

I held up a board that said "Number 433" and was photographed standing in front of a wall facing front and sideways. It was the so-called mug shot for criminal records. I did not have any thoughts or feelings. After my glasses were confiscated, everything looked hazy. Holding a plastic spoon and two bowls that the guard had given me, I followed him to the cell to which I was assigned.

God's Will for Leading Me to Prison

I entered the cell and despite my thick cloudy vision, I began noticing people's faces all turned toward me. At that moment, someone shouted, "Turn around and sit facing the wall!"

I did not know why, but I sat facing the wall for a long time. I found out later that it was part of being initiated into the cell. After a long time, I heard the same voice again.

"Now turn around, and tell us your name, address, occupation, the nature of your crime, and your prior record – in the order as it reads on this piece of paper."

So I turned around, and after saying "Hello" in a loud voice, I introduced myself according to the list, including the nature of my crime. As they listened to my story, they began to whisper to each other. Then I heard a comment, "That doesn't sound like something you should be arrested for. Something sounds wrong."

"They arrested an acting university president even before the final verdict had been reached? That seems unfair!"

Everyone had his own opinion regarding my crime. Then again, I heard someone saying in a loud voice, "That Handong Global University is a problem school!"

They all seemed knowledgeable about the law as if they were attorneys. Then a man who appeared to be the leader in the cell asked me, "President, have you had lunch?"

Only then did I realize that I had skipped lunch. It was already past four o'clock in the afternoon.

"Hey, bring him a piece of bread!"

The next day, I told this story to my wife who came to visit me. She asked, "Did you eat the bread?"

"Of course I did! It was very good and I was hungry." I smiled. My wife did not know whether to laugh or cry, wondering how I could have peace of mind to eat in such a situation.

My fellow cellmates were very considerate of me. There were two small tables in the room and the cell leader allowed me to put my bowl on one of them. He also exempted me from clean-up duties. At 9 pm, it was time to sleep. I wondered how all these men could sleep in such a small room. Each person rolled his blanket into a pillow, and 35 men were arranged in order. Every other man lay down with his head facing the opposite way. We were all lying on our sides so that our noses almost touched the feet of the men lying next to us. We were literally like sardines in a can.

According to the prison rule, we slept with the lights on. With such bright lights on, everyone seemed to have a difficult time falling asleep. The room leader spoke up and said, "Let us each share how we lived in the outside world."

Everyone shared about how they regretted their lives and how they should not have done this or that so they would not end up in prison. Finally, it came to my turn.

"I don't have much to say, but could I sing instead? My hometown is in an isolated rural region, now submerged by the construction of a dam. So I'm a wanderer without a hometown, and I like this song called, "The Spring of My Hometown"."

"You want to sing? Go ahead."

I began to sing in a low voice, a song that I learned in elementary school.

Flowers bloomed in my hometown, long time ago.

Peaches, apples and apricots… and pink blossoms too.

Red and violet of the rainbow, flowers paint the town.

I still long to go back to my hometown in the sun.

New village of flower is my old hometown.

Wind blows from the south to the blue field.

At the stream the weeping willow danced in my neighborhood.

I long to go back to the days when I played in the midst.

Soon all the prison family started to sing along with me. When I finished singing, I felt something hot in my throat. I heard the sound of tears falling from around the cell. As soon as I ended my singing, the leader of the room said, "Hmm, President Kim, you sing pretty well."

The atmosphere changed because of singing. The song that everybody learned in their elementary schools became the bond of friendship with my cell-mates on that first night in prison. People seemed to briefly forget their depression and the fact that they were in confinement. I closed my eyes and thought of the mountains in my hometown. All of a sudden, something burst inside my heart and I could not hold back my tears as I thought, I'm now 62 years old. How did I end up in a place like this?

Lying down in that cell filled with 35 men placed side by side, I stood before God as a bare, naked soul. Honestly I did not know what to think for a couple of days. I had been so busy trying my best to lead the school, but never thought that I would end up in prison.

Then I started to think about God's will for letting me come to prison.

"Commit your way to the Lord: trust in him and he will do this: He will make your righteousness shine like the dawn, the justice of your cause like the noonday sun. Be still before the LORD and wait patiently for him; do not fret when men succeed in their ways, when they carry out their wicked schemes." (Psalms 37:5-7)

God did not call us to be the lord of our own lives, but to trust Him as our Lord. So right then and there, I believed and prayed that my Lord God would continue to take hold of me and the school until the end.

"Be still, and know that I am God; I will be exalted among the nations, I will be exalted in the earth." (Psalms 46:10)

Experiencing True Freedom

I realized that prison was a world with real people and that it was a bearable place. Each person in that place was born with a precious life. Each person's life had its own circumstances, tears, sighs, and sorrows which only that individual could tell. Each man was searching for his own hope.

Three days into my imprisonment, in the morning of Teacher's Day of May 15, 2001, the prison guard asked me discretely, "President Kim, haven't you heard any news?"

"How can I hear any outside news when I'm sitting here inside the high prison walls?" I answered.

"Thousands of Handong students are coming here in honor of Teacher's Day. The prison officers are preparing for a state of emergency and everyone seems nervous. I'm a little worried, too."

"I'm sure nothing will happen. Our students are mature and wise," I answered.

Sometime later, Yu-Kang Choi, the president of student council and other student representatives came to visit me. They began to weep as soon as they saw me.

"President Kim, this must be hard for you. Right now, there are about 1,800 students, professors, and parents outside that came in 29 buses. They are singing "The Teacher's Song" for you and the vice president towards this building."

I was in tears, too, as I heard them. And I told the

students, "Do not show any anger or agitation and be diligent in your studies and in lectures."

That afternoon, the prison guard came to me with a bright face.

"President Kim, you've really educated your students well. They finished their Teacher's Day event in complete order. They left a huge pile of carnations in honor of you outside the prison wall. When they left, there wasn't a single speck of trash left behind. If all our citizens act this way, I would have nothing to worry about. I've never been so moved in my 20 years as a prison guard."

I cannot tell you how proud I was of our students at that moment.

> "But he knows the way that I take; when he has tested me, I will come forth as gold." (Job 23:10)

I wrote my feelings in my journal that day:
Dear God, I stand before you right now absolutely

powerless. I never stood before You without worrying about my name, reputation, pride, and popularity. Although I'm experiencing pain and sadness, I've thrown off everything and am enjoying true freedom.

Until now, I lived my life running toward You, but You have momentarily stopped me. In this special place, in a special way, You freed me and are meeting me one on one. This place is where I belong. This place will be my upper room where I will meet my Lord.

After a week of imprisonment, I was moved to a cell with only seven people. Everyone in that cell was a newcomer, so I did not have to go through another initiation. Only then was I able to focus on each person in my cell. I wrote out the Lord's Prayer and the Apostle's Creed for each person and I suggested that we give thanks to God for each meal. Strangely, no one objected.

I prayed whenever someone had to appear in court. In this way, I was able to calm my heart and share

God's grace with my cellmates each day. For seven years, I had not had a day of rest or had been free from worrying about money. It was nice to be able to finally meditate on the Bible without such financial concerns. I read all the books that I wanted to read before. I had nothing to do except to pray and sing praises while I was in prison. I began to think that perhaps God was giving me a special vacation since I had been so busy up to that point. In that cell, I prayed the prayer of Jabez for Handong every day.

"Oh, that you would bless me (Handong) and enlarge my (Handong's) territory! Let your hand be with me (Handong) and keep me (Handong) from harm so that I (Handong) will be free from pain." (1 Chronicles 4:10)

Four weeks into my imprisonment at Kyongju Prison, on May 28, 2011, the warden came to me and said, "You'll be moved to Daegu Prison in preparation for the Appellate Court trial there. So be ready by

10 o'clock tomorrow morning."

When I thought about leaving the next day, my heart was in turmoil over my cellmates with whom I had been living for almost three weeks. On the morning of my departure, I held each person's hands and earnestly prayed with them. I cried and they cried too.

"Father God, thank You for allowing us to meet here. We are in a tough place, but even a prison becomes a place of peace and thanksgiving because You are here with us. Have mercy on these men and bless them so they may become Your children. Let them become bearers of the evidence that You are with us on this earth. Watch over them as the apple of Your eye. Protect their families. If they have to stay here a long time, let them learn of a new life through patience and let their faith grow."

One of the cellmates there sent a letter to Handong after he was released:

"How have you been? I spent a month with President Kim in May 2001 while he was in Kyongju Prison. I'd like to tell you about the man whom I saw and experienced firsthand. The month that I spent with President Kim was a truly precious period of my time. He always started and ended each day in prayer. He seemed more like a nice man living next door than a university president. After watching him never losing his smile and always living in prayer, even during his difficult times in prison, I, too, repented of my own life. He stayed up late into the night reading all the countless letters that the school sent him each day, reading every word on each page.

I still remember that day. The morning of the day when he was to be transferred to Daegu Prison, he knelt down and prayed with tears. He prayed for Handong rather than for himself and he cried as he prayed for all his students. I do not know all the details of the incident, but I thought he was an incredible man because he showed no resentment toward anyone. To everyone at Handong, I ask that you write many letters to encourage President Kim and send him hope. I think all of you are lucky to be attending Handong, where President Kim is the captain."

Embracing the Heart of Jesus

The day I was leaving Kyongju Prison, my cellmates and I all said our good-byes in tears. When I came outside with my sack, other prisoners who were to be transferred to Daegu Prison were lined up and roped, like a string of dead fish. My hands were cuffed and a thick rope bound me from shoulder to waist, front and back. I could hardly move because the handcuffs were so tight on my wrists, and I could not even lean back on my chair because of the thick rope across my back.

Then, the warden came to me and said,

"President Kim, please understand. We have a new regulation after the recent escape incident. We are now required to put two handcuffs on each prisoner."

His caring words touched me, and my eyes filled up with tears. The bus left Kyongju Prison and headed for Daegu Prison on Highway 1. The mountains and fields were covered with lush summer green and all seemed new to me. Before I realized it, there were tears running down my face. It was not because of the pain that I felt, but suddenly I pictured Jesus Christ walking up the hill of Golgotha with a crown of thorns on His head.

"For even the Son of Man did not come to be served, but to serve, and to give his life as a ransom for many." (Mark 10:45)

As I found myself bound in cuffs, the weight of the pain our Lord had to endure broke my heart. Jesus Christ, who is God, came to this world as a man and endured the crown of thorns, the whips, the insults, and carried the cross to pay the price of my sins! God the Creator was persecuted by His own creatures! But

I, the true sinner, am traveling so comfortably on this bus.

As I meditated on the love of God who sent His only Son to die for me, a sinner, I cried because I was so thankful and because I felt so sorry.

I was indebted to the immeasurable love of God displayed through the sacrifice of Jesus Christ! The more I meditated on Jesus who carried the weight of this world and suffered for my sins, the more the road to Daegu drew me into a place of deeper grace.

> "Who shall separate us from the love of Christ? Shall trouble or hardship or persecution or famine or nakedness or danger or sword? No, in all these things we are more than conquerors through him who loved us." (Romans 8:35, 37)

As I passed the prison office, some of the prison guards who had been reading the newspapers looked up and recognized me, and asked,

"Are you the President Young-Gil Kim of Han-dong Global University? You are also the chairman of the Korea Association for Creation Research, right? We were just reading about you in the newspapers."

They were members of the Christian Mustard Seed at Daegu Prison.

"We read the news article about the event Han-dong students prepared on Teacher's Day. If you were guilty of anything, the students, staff and faculty members would have been the first ones to protest against you."

Once we arrived at Daegu Prison, I was sent to a single cell for "convicted" prisoners. Being in a private cell, I was able to sing hymns and meditate on the Bible. I took the hymnal, which my wife had sent, and sang page by page. When I came across the song "Sound of Love Bell," written by Seok-Gyun Kim, I felt that it was a musical poem written for Handong Global University. I changed the lyrics from "Sound of Love Bell" to "Sound of Handong Bell" and sang it every day.

Only after some time did I realize that Mr. Kim's son, Joo-Hun, was a Handong student. I dreamt of the day when I would stand with the original songwriter during Handong chapel and sing this song with him. Later, after my release, I took private lessons from my daughter-in-law who majored in violin to learn the right melody. However, even with my hard effort I always made mistakes. After I was released, the day finally came for me to sing in chapel with Mr. Seok-Gyun Kim. When we sang a duet I made the same mistake, but he comforted me saying, "President Kim, you sang the right melody and I made a mistake." We were both deeply touched, and with teary eyes we heartedly sang "Sound of Handong Bell" together.

I am praying, Lord, for Your great grace

So that Handong's borders may be expanded all over the world.

Oh Lord, wash off all our transgressions with

Your precious blood.

Let us be one in the love of God,

Together in faith, together in hope.

We go hand in hand together in love.

Oh Lord, the sound of love bells

Wrap around all the people of Handong.

I am praying, Lord, for Your great grace

So that You spare and use Handong greatly.

Oh Lord, let Your new light shine upon the darkness of our hearts.

Let us obey Your word of truth.

Together in tolerance, together in embrace

To the Lord we go together in love.

Oh Lord, the sound of love bells

Wraps around all the people of Handong.

About a month after my transfer to Daegu Prison, a Christian guard came to me and said, "We think that you are going to leave this place soon and so we have prepared a special event tonight. Please join us and share your testimony with us."

And so in the Christian prison gathering, I preached a sermon titled "Your Attitude Should Be the Same as Jesus" (Philippians 2:5-11). After the message, they put their hands on my shoulders and earnestly prayed for me.

"We, the Church of Smyrna in this prison send you, Elder Young-Gil Kim, as a missionary to the outside world." Their tears fell on my shoulders and hands.

"President Kim, when you are released into the outside world, please don't forget us, the Church of Smyrna."

To this day, I still remind myself, "I am a missionary sent by the Church of Smyrna."

On July 4, 2001, 53 days into my imprisonment in Kyongju and Daegu Prison, I was released on bail along with Vice President Sung-Yeon Oh.

Five months passed, and on December 28, 2001 the appeal trial in the Daegu Appellate Court was scheduled to be held at 10 o'clock in the morning. The trial that had begun in early spring continued through the dead heat of the summer and was finally coming to an end in the winter with the final verdict. There had been a total of five trials including the final one. The last trial was going to determine whether I got to retain the presidency of Handong Global University.

The night before the final verdict, I prayed to God. Oh Lord, if it is Your will that I should lead Your school, please allow me to be acquitted.

Many Handong parents, students, and professors were already gathered outside waiting for the court session to begin. It was a clear day, but a gusty, chilly, December wind was blowing through the court grounds, kicking up dust as if wanting to sweep away all our past trials and hardships.

In the front of Courtroom 41, several hundreds of parents were waiting for me and the courtroom was jam-packed. As the appointed hour approached, the room was filled with dead silence to the point that one could hear a pin drop. Nobody could anticipate the final verdict. The few minutes that we waited for the judges to enter the room seemed like hours. Finally, with an order for everyone to rise, the judges entered the courtroom.

After dealing with other cases that were minor, my case number was called and the presiding judge took about 10 minutes to read the final verdict. While the verdict was being read, my mind quickly replayed with mixed emotions the very phone call inviting me to become the founding president of Handong Global University to the day of my final verdict.

Ultimately, the chief justice declared solemnly "NOT GUILTY" of the major offenses and issued a fine for the minor charges. The trial was closed. I thanked God as I wiped tears from my cheeks. Many others in the Handong family who came to support me were also weeping. Attorney Jong-Soon Lee, who took on this case pro bono, told us that this verdict was a 120 percent victory for Handong Global University. Father God, You have taken a heavy burden from me! Thank you!

"He will judge your people in righteousness, your afflicted ones with justice." (Psalms 72:2)

Chapter 2

Action and Reaction
God's Drama,
Restoring the Fallen World

Spiritual Law
vs. Scientific Law

The first words of the Bible declare that God is the Creator of the universe, who rules over the world and human history.

> "In the beginning, God created the heavens and the earth." (Genesis 1:1)

While studying the first chapter of Genesis, I learned the Hebrew meanings of "creation" in Genesis 1:1. We must not be confused in two different words which are originally used and hidden in the word "creation." One is "bara" and the other is "asa". The word "creation" in Hebrew is "bara," means the creation from nothing to something ("ex-nihilo"). When the word "bara" becomes a verb within a sentence, the subject is always the Almighty Creator God. God created time itself and God transcends time. God is timeless in His being. He is the only initiator to move the first thing. Meanwhile, the Hebrew word "asa" means a transformation of existing materials. Unfortunately, this distinction in the Hebrew language can easily get lost in the English translation. The words "Bara" and "Asa" give us clearer understanding about the infinite nature of our Creator God (BARA) and the creature that is finite (ASA). As to a spiritual being, God seems invisible to our eyes; however, He reveals Himself only through His own creation.

"For since the creation of the world God's invisible qualities—his eternal power and divine nature—have been clearly seen, being understood from what has been made, so that men are without excuse." (Romans 1:20)

The visible natural world reveals the invisible spiritual world. The invisible spiritual world can only be understood through faith. In other words, the visible world is the manifestation of the invisible world. The natural and supernatural worlds are not two separate worlds, but the same world expressed in different forms.[16]

When we watch a movie, we are moved by the pictures displayed in front of our eyes. However, in order to produce a film, it undergoes a complicated process which includes planning, script writing, filming, recording, editing, marketing, and so on. We cannot deny the reality of these processes just because we cannot see them.

> "By faith we understand that the universe was formed at God's command, so that what is seen was not made out of what was visible." (Hebrews 11:3)

Science vs. Miracle

Many secular people accept and believe only in the existence of a visible world. But invisible does not mean something is nonexistent.[17] The invisible is invisible simply because it is in the spiritual world. The mental or spiritual world is outside the scientific realm.

"God created both: the visible, natural, material world, as well as the invisible, supernatural, spiritual world." (Colossians 1:16)

The hierarchy of created worlds is shown in the figure following. In the visible physical natural world, there are four levels; the lowest is the atomic level, then, plant, animal, and the highest of these is the human level. The fifth and the highest level of them all is the supernatural, invisible, and spiritual level.

After the Fall, the heavenly spiritual world and the

physical world were separated. The invisible spiritual world can be understood only by faith on the revealed words in the Bible. We could not understand the invisible spiritual reality through our visible scientific knowledge. The cross is the only way to connect the gap and restore the broken relationship between God

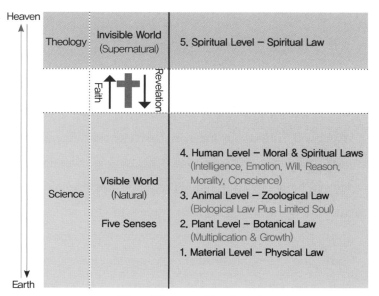

Five different worlds of creation

and human beings.

Just as there are natural scientific laws in the physical world, spiritual laws exist in the spiritual world. God ordained order and laws for each of the worlds and levels. For example, at the level of atoms, the laws of physics govern the rotation of electrons around protons. God created biological laws for living things, such as growth and multiplication. In the human world, God gave spiritual and moral laws.

Unlike animals, God breathed spirit into human beings and gave the Ten Commandments as laws to keep. God specifies the spiritual relation between humans and Himself in the first four Commandments while the latter six Commandments deal with moral laws to be observed in human relationships. Humans are able to lift up in worship prayers to God who is spirit, through spirit. Another function of the human spirit is to maintain conscience. Conscience is a general moral capacity that God has given to every human being. Since animals do not have spirits, they can neither have an object of worship nor a conscience. As a result, they are not able to repent of their sins. However, when human beings commit sin, they are convicted by their conscience.

As the spiritual laws of the spiritual world, the first to fourth Commandments are the highest set of laws that govern all other laws of this world. However, the laws of the invisible world also govern the visible, natural world.

Scientific research can be defined as an effort to find explanations to the natural laws of this world. It deals with the physical world that can be detected through the five senses or by scientific instruments. The goal of scientific researchers is to discover new phenomena, order, processes, and laws of this universe based on pre-existing information such as scientific laws, order, harmony and genetic information of the physical world.

On the other hand, a miracle is an event which cannot be understood by scientific reasoning within the same realm of time and place of the actual event. Thus, a miracle precedes the realm of science.

When I try to raise a stone with my hand, I cannot violate or ignore the law of gravity acting on the stone. The reason that I can raise the stone is because the law of gravity is overcome by the greater force of my muscle. A stone cannot raise itself by its own volition. However, if the stone was raised by an invisible force, we may consider such an incident as a miracle. In order for us to accept miracles, it requires a quantum jump or leap from the limits of our five senses to understand the higher realm of the supernatural world. There is no conflict between science and miracles and they are not contradictory to each other. In fact, they are compatible and mutually complementary.[18]

As a scientist, I once believed that a miracle is a scientifically impossible event. However, I came to embrace the reality that Jesus turning water into wine and feeding a group of several thousand people with just five loaves of bread and two fish were clearly miraculous events that left no room for any scientific explanation (John 2:9, Matthew 14:19).

Turning water into wine can be seen as a miracle to human beings, but it is a natural event in the supernatural world when God intervenes. If animals were to observe the human world, everything would seem like a miracle. All human activities such as driving a car, flying on an airplane, reading a newspaper or working on a computer would be considered miracles to our pets. But for us, all these are normal activities. They are natural products of scientific research. Just as the events that are considered miracles in the lower level world are actually common sense in the higher level world, the miracles described in the Bible are more than possible if God intervenes. Miraculous events are a normal result in the hands of our Creator God who designed and spoke all things into being.

Miracles lie outside the realm of natural science. The acceptance of miracles in the Bible depends on the level of one's spiritual knowledge and faith. It primarily depends on whether or not one believes and accepts the existence of the Almighty God, our Creator. The miracles Jesus performs in the Bible are not subjects of scientific investigation or interpretation, but a set of powerful evidences declaring the truth that Jesus Christ Himself is the Creator of the universe!

While on this earth, Jesus Christ performed many miracles, and the miraculous event of His resurrection stands at the peak of His life and ministry. When we believe in the Creator God, we should have no issues with believing in all of Jesus' miracles, including His resurrection.

"Through him all things were made; without him nothing was made that has been made." (John 1:3)

God-Centered Life vs. Humanism

Why must a Syntropy Drama be played out in this

world? In the history of human thought, "God-centered life" and human-centered "humanism" make up two big mountains. At the time of creation, the creation order of this earth was perfect and the relationship between God and man was intimate. Human beings lived a God-centered life in direct communication and obedience to God's command. However, ever since man's disobedience to God's command, the relationship with God has been broken. This caused the gradual and steady destruction of the creation order by moving from a God-centered life to a human-centered life.

Humanism is a life that is human-centered and far from a relationship with God. With the help of Greek civilization, its influence began to spread even to Hebraism and the birthplace of Christian philosophy, Jerusalem.

Greeks also had gods, but not the Almighty Creator God. Their gods were merely an extension or reproduction of human beings and they only existed for human beings.

The only interest of Greek civilization was the pursuit of human-centered happiness. In his works, Aristotle stated that the pursuit of happiness is the highest good for man. The Greeks had no interest in the afterlife, which caused them to focus on enjoying the existing world. They also embraced rationalism, which emphasized theoria (Greek for contemplation), observing an object from a distance to gain understanding. However, rationalism attempted to apply this standard of reasoning beyond the visible world and measure the existence of an invisible God and spirit.

Ancient Greek culture seemed to lose influence as a result of the rise of the Roman Empire. However, it was actually passed on to Italy during the 14th century through the crusaders of the Eastern Roman Empire based in Constantinople and spread to the entire European region. This became the foundation of the birth of modern science and the Age of Enlightenment in the 17th and 18th centuries. This Age of Enlighten-

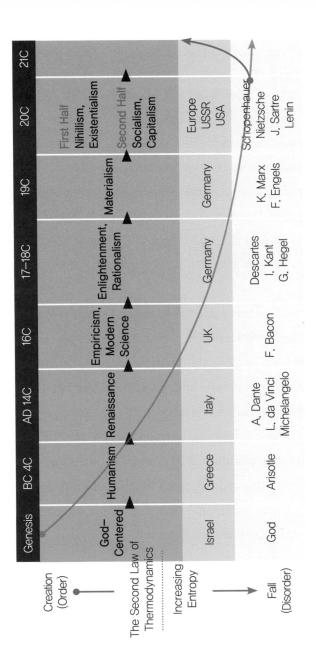

Historical changes of human thoughts

ment further developed into modernism among the Europeans and became the predominant pattern of thought in the 19th and 20th centuries. Humanity left God and replaced Him with rational thinking and self-centeredness. This is the reemergence of humanism where man is the principal agent. Consequently, numerous philosophers and thinkers influenced the entire world with ideas and thoughts rooted in humanism.

René Descartes (1569-1650) was a French philosopher, mathematician and rationalist. He considered human knowledge as the basis for truth. As an advocate of rationalistic epistemology, he believed that the first precept was never to accept a thing as true until I knew it as such without a single doubt. He opened the door for allowing truth to be determined solely by human knowledge and judgment. Through his influence, society came to deny the existence of the unperceivable supernatural spiritual world.

According to empiricism, an approach introduced

by the Enlightenment philosopher, John Locke (1632-1704) believed that knowledge came only from sensory experience. Francis Bacon (1561-1626) contributed to the development of science through his scientific approach to empiricism. But his dependence on experiments and experiences led to the denial of the existence of God who transcends experiments and experiences. Furthermore, he denied the human spirit in man created in God's image.

Immanuel Kant (1724-1804) considered morality and ethics as his academic goal and became a successor to the Greek philosophers (Socrates, Plato, and Aristotle). However, by placing the human mind at the core of knowledge, he drove God out of the human world. He was the first post-Middle Ages philosopher to define God as an unrecognizable entity. This caused him to deny all supernatural miracles recorded in the Bible and set the ground for liberal theology by placing theological discussions within the limits of human knowledge. He strongly believed that even though people may never know God's presence empirically, they are justified in believing in God for the sake of morality.

Georg Wilhelm Friedrich Hegel (1770-1831) was a German philosopher and a major figure in German idealism. His philosophy dominated Germany in the 19th century. Instead of viewing the Bible as a true record of historical accounts, Hegel considered it to be a myth or a historical story. He saw the biblical accounts of the creation or the birth of Jesus Christ as stories. He rejected God's creation and providence and argued for materialism which was later passed on to Karl Heinrich Marx (1818-1883) and Friedrich Engels (1820-1895). Hegel believed that the human mind was the only truth. Because of this, he considered all religion and God to be a product of the activity of the mind and denied the existence of God.

Another German philosopher who lived in the same age as Hegel Ludwig was Andreas Feuerbach (1804-1872). He advocated for materialism. In contrast to Hegel, who took the human mind as the test for truth, Feuerbach placed the standard of truth in objects. This idea was further systematized by Karl Marx. Karl Marx argued that the universe emerges from and is rooted in material. He introduced this idea by using the dialectic approach to explain matter in motion, evolution, and development. He argued that such dialectical motion and evolutionary development of matter formed the human world, culture and history. In 1859, Marx's materialism was reinforced by the theory of evolution which was introduced by Charles Robert Darwin (1809-1882) from England.

The 19th century was a turbulent time of changes in ideas where the standard of judgment transferred from God's revelation to humanity and, once again, to material or matter. Influenced by Hegel's philosophy, Karl Marx's ideas and Darwin's theory of evolution, the latter half of the 19th century developed into an atheistic society with humanity becoming the foundational entity. As a result of atheism, humanity was removed from God and this developed into Arthur Schopenhauer's (1778-1860) nihilism. Schopenhauer viewed humanity to have an aimless will to live, which he considered to be evil and meaningless. This resulted in his pessimism. To him, humanity which left God in distrust resulted in losing all purpose for existence and was left with an aimless will to life and futility.

Friedrich Wilhelm Nietzsche (1844-1900) was an atheist who was influenced by the works of Schopenhauer. Consequently he viewed humanity as having an aimless will to live. However, in contrast to Schopenhauer, he had an extremely optimistic view of humanity and advocated for will power. Nietzsche's philosophy of life denied pessimism while supporting absolute positivity. He also harshly criticized the idea of love and Christian values by defining them as slave morality followed by the weak. He argued for a strong master morality that went beyond a view of humanity as a source of love. He was also opposed to Hegel's mental philosophy and claimed will philosophy. Another philosophical concept introduced by Nietzsche, who argued for overall positivity in life, was the philosophy of Ubermensch (German for "overman"). As a result of his extreme affirmation in the master morality of humanity, the world entered into racism and imperialism in the 20th century.

Existentialism, introduced by Søren Kierkegaard (1813-1855), governed much of the philosophical thinking of the 20th century. Other existentialists were Jean Paul Sartre (1905-1980) and Martin Heidegger (1889-1976). Kierkegaard was born into a Lutheran family in Copenhagen, Denmark. Although he had completed his theological study at the age of 27, he did not receive ordination to become a pastor. He criticized Hegel's idealism as being nothing more than abstract thinking, and emphasized existential values that focused on the living human individual and character. The aim of existential philosophy and theology was for an individual to return to his original place and find restoration of his true essence.

Existential philosophy centers on the effort of an individual being to discover his true essence. The background and philosophical thinking of existentialism can also be defined as the individual's effort to recover and return to his true essence or purpose of existence. It also means that the individual must overcome his current self to find true freedom. In other words, the main focus of the existentialist is on the individual's effort to find his true essence by overcoming current anxiety and crisis. However, existentialism does not accept God's creation, the fall of man, the salvation of Jesus Christ, and eternal life.

Communism is also another form of existentialism. The word "communism," which comes from the Latin word "communis," is a social system of common wealth. While communism follows the same thoughts of existentialism, it is completely different in its methodology of discovering and restoring the individual. Communism is based on a mechanical world view of materialistic dialectic which emphasizes physical revolution as a solution to discovering the individual being. This opened up the door to the approval of purges. This modern philosophy embraced the realities that humanity faced as the only significant problem and also denied the existence of God and the Bible.

Entering into the 18th century, the English industrial revolution and the French political revolution led the way to the establishment of the liberal democratic market economy system in Europe. However, the seriousness of social issues only increased as surplus wealth was distributed to the higher class and equal distribution of wealth failed. Under these circumstances, Karl Marx, at the age of 30, formed the communist league with 28-year old Engels and together published the Communist Manifesto in 1848.

Vladimir Ilyich Lenin (1870-1924) embraced communism and applied it in all areas of politics, economy, and society through the Russian Revolution in

October of 1917. Also known as Leninism, it was a revolutionary theory led by the proletariat class. Then in 1991, with the dissolution of the Soviet Union after 74 years, the non-productivity and inefficiency of communism were confirmed. Other communist nations such as China also abandoned the pure form of communism by accepting various aspects of capitalism, particularly its market approach to the economy.[19]

In this way, human thoughts were corrupted into humanism, rationalism, materialism and secularism after the fall. Through this process of change in ideas, the element of education also transitioned naturally from being God-centered to human-centered. Ideas were indoctrinated through education and indoctrinated education changed ideas. The surprising fact is that due to the influence of these ideas, the materialistic world view began to govern even the invisible spiritual world of God. Humanity's attempt to explain the invisible spiritual world and the existence of God which can only be found through God's Word, the Bible with only what is visible, increased confusion and caused the intensification of materialism.

Law of Grace vs. Law of Gravitation

There are two great laws operating in this universe: the law of gravitation that governs the visible and physical world and the law of grace that governs the invisible spiritual world.[20]

The law of gravitation is selfish and human-centered. In contrast, the law of grace is a God-centered life which shares the love of God that is freely given to us without limitation. The main purpose of life in the secular world is to enlarge the gravitational field by maximizing the force of gravity in pursuit of the material riches in the visible world. But true Christian leadership is the way of life that gives up one's visible things and pursues the invisible, which gives more eternal value of the spiritual world.

Human beings are naturally governed by the law of gravitation and we are trapped in the gravitational field which seeks after self-gain. But the grace and love of Jesus who died on the cross broke this law of gravitation. Jesus' gift of forgiveness through His grace is the most astonishing miracle of all the miracles He performed for humans. The only reason grace is freely given to us is because the Giver Himself allowed His own Son to pay for the whole price of our sins on the cross.

We tend to easily accept and have confidence in the laws operating in His created natural world, such as the law of gravitation, the law of energy, and the law of genetics. But we often reject the spiritual laws of God for our family, society, and nations.

Christians who have experienced the love of God must learn to live according to the standards in keeping the laws of God. God rules directly in the physical world. In the areas of politics, laws, economy, culture and society, however, God rules indirectly, entrusting human beings with the task of practicing justice and serving in love.

Nevertheless, since the Fall of Man, we have begun to disobey God's laws. However, despite our sins, God has been gracious enough to offer His universal grace to all His creation. In other words, it is His covenant was renewed and restored for all His creation (Genesis 3:15).

It is very important for Christians to focus exclusively on the spiritual things, or Bible studies, and evangelical campaigns, while turning a blind eye to the distinctive tension of contemporary life. We must show the world that Christianity is more than the salvation of individuals. Only the message of the cross presents us with the path of faith to gain a comprehensive understanding of the physical, moral and spiritual orders of the entire universe.

The Creation vs. the Fall

God's ultimate purpose of creating the universe is for it to reveal His glory. What is the glory of God? It is Him "Being God." Where is the glory of God? Everything created by God reflects His glory. In nature, we learn that God is creative, wise, organized and powerful. He enjoys variety and loves beauty.

"The heavens declare the glory of God; the skies proclaim the works of his hands. Day after day they pour forth speech; night after night they reveal knowledge. They have no speech they use no words; no sound is heard from them. Yet their voice goes out into all the earth, their words to the ends of the world. In the heavens God has pitched a tent for the sun." (Psalms 19:1-4)

It is God who directs the lives of His creatures. Since we were created, there is no way that we can understand the purpose of our creation in our own strength. If we were to see an invention for the first time, we would not know its purpose and/or how to use it. In the same way, the invention itself would not be able to discern the purpose of its existence. Only the Creator or the user manual could reveal its purpose. Therefore, it is only in God that we discover our origin, identity, meaning, purpose, and calling.[21] Everyone's life is under God's authority.

When God created human beings, He distinguished us from the rest of His creation by creating us uniquely.

"So God created mankind in his own image, in the image of God he created them; male and female he created them." (Genesis 1:27)

"Then the LORD God formed a man from the dust of the ground and breathed into his nostrils the breath of life, and the man became a living being." (Genesis 2:7)

The Bible declares that God created the universe and created human beings in His own image. He also established the moral rules and order for our lives. Genesis Chapter 1 writes that when God created the heavens and the earth, the created order in the universe was perfect. But, after the Fall of Man through disobedience of God's commands, we became alienated from God with our conscience becoming paralyzed, and intelligence losing its direction. This ultimately led to the destruction of God's creation order. Therefore, all men have sinned (Romans 3:23), resulting in eternal death.

But the love of God yearned to find a way to pay for the price of human sin. God wants to restore this world into a God-centered world that seeks after eternal things. God's justice cannot tacitly agree with sin nor forgive sin without a full payment of the penalty of our sins. But the love of God desires to forgive all sins. There is no single person in all of human history who could pay the penalty for his or her sins to satisfy the justice of God because human beings are born as sinners. A condemned criminal cannot pay the penalty of another condemned criminal. Only a true human being who is without sin is able to pay off the penalty for human sins. Being conceived through the Holy Spirit, Jesus was the only man who was free from sin. In other words, the Incarnation of God was the only way to qualify for the requirements of salvation to forgive the sins of man.

Whenever I am given an opportunity to speak at testimonial seminars or creation science lectures, I often use the imagery of a judgmental court scene to explain why the Father God had to provide a way for His own Son for His atonement. Let's say the defendant murderer was the judge's one and only son. Because he loves his son, he would want to release his son with an acquittal. If he is a righteous judge, he would have to sentence his own son to the death penalty. Being a judge who could not neglect his responsibility and duty, he pronounces the death sentence in great pain.

Then the judge takes off his robe and speaks as he steps into the defendant's deck. I will pour all my curse and death penalty over to my son in Calvary. By the death sentence of the High Court Judgment, Jesus, His only Son, was sent and carried a very heavy cross to the hill of Calvary. There, He was stripped, nailed and pierced. God did not look on His own beloved Son on the cross ("Father, why do you forsake me?"), but rather, poured down all His hatred of sin toward all mankind. Thus He made His own Son pay the penalty in full until He was satisfied.

We, human beings, who had no way of escaping death were only able to escape it because of the Father's love.

"The law requires that nearly everything be cleansed with blood, and without the shedding of blood there is no forgiveness." (Hebrews 9:22)

The most dramatic event in the history of the universe was that the Creator God came to this earth in human form, and died on the cross to save us from our sins. At the same time, God was able to justify His distinctive characters of love and justice with Jesus Christ, who Himself was God, chose to die on the cross to pay for our sins. Isn't this the secret of the Gospel, God's amazing grace?

"For God so loved the world that he gave his one and only Son, that whoever believes in him shall not perish but have eternal life." (John 3:16)

Why does God love us? He does not love us because of what we are now, but what we are now. It is because He created us and redeemed us through His love. There is nothing we have to do except to receive the Father's love and to remain in it. Since the grace was given to us once and for all, we are to accept the free gift with thanksgiving.

"For it is by grace you have been saved, through faith—and this is not from yourselves, it is the gift of God—not by works, so that no one can boast." (Ephesians 2:8-9)

Because of the sin of man, our universe became corrupted. In order to bring restoration to this entropy-increasing world, God already planned the syntropy project.

"And I will put enmity between you and the woman, and between your offspring and hers; he will crush your head, and you will strike his heel." (Genesis 3:15)

Since the Fall of Man (Genesis 3:3-6) the world has turned into a spiritual battleground with two invisible powers contending for the same territory.

God's adversary, Satan, who invaded creation to lead humanity to its fall, is now doing everything in his power to hold the territories he has occupied. But,

God has launched a counterattack to reclaim His rightful domain. With His death, Jesus Christ has paid the price for the sin of man in full and has already won victory through His resurrection.[22]

We, who have been saved by the grace of God, are called as His soldiers in this ongoing spiritual battle. The fighting may be fierce but as soldiers for Christ, we must never give up because our fight is essentially a mop-up operation in a victorious battle. Our boldness comes from knowing the final outcome of the game in advance.

This world is the stage where the victorious drama of Jesus Christ against sin and death, hell and Satan is going to unfold. God has given each and every one of the characters that appears on the stage a unique role. As the people of God, we should now obey the commands of our Lord who saved us. It is fulfilling His vision to save the lost and rebuild this fallen world.

We have been called as witnesses for Jesus Christ to proclaim the power of love and transformation in this broken and chaotic world. This power of love and transformation must start from us and spread into families, friends, communities, and the rest of the world. This is when we will be able to fulfill the Syntropy Drama of rebuilding our foundations that have been destroyed over generations.

"Stand firm then, with the belt of truth buckled around your waist, with the breastplate of righteousness in place, and with your feet fitted with the readiness that comes from the gospel of peace. In addition to all this, take up the shield of faith, with which you can extinguish all the flaming arrows of the evil one. Take the helmet of salvation and the sword of the Spirit, which is the word of God. And pray in the Spirit on all occasions with all kinds of prayers and requests. With this in mind, be alert and always keep on praying for all the saints." (Ephesians 6:14-18)

> This world is the stage where the victorious drama of Jesus Christ against sin and death, hell and Satan is going to unfold. God has given each and every one of the characters that appears on the stage a unique role. It is fulfilling His vision to save the lost and rebuild this fallen world.

PART TWO

The Law of Syntropy II

Action, from Disorder to Order

Chapter 3

Handong Global University,
the Stage of Syntropy Drama

Syntropy Leadership: Nehemiah

I read the book of Nehemiah several times in order to develop an educational structure for global Christian leadership that will change the world. It was the last account recorded in the Old Testament on the restoration of the broken walls of Jerusalem. Furthermore, it describes the spiritual restoration of the nation of Israel. As I read Nehemiah, I earnestly prayed that Handong Global University would produce many global Christian leaders in the 21st century with the commitment and sincerity of Nehemiah.

Nehemiah led the Israelites home to Jerusalem after the Babylonian Empire fell to the Persians. His purpose was to rebuild the broken wall and to bring spiritual restoration to Israel. Among all the people, why did God choose Nehemiah—the cupbearer to a gentile king—as the leader? The title of cupbearer was only given to a person whom the king could trust with his life. Just by his title we can see Nehemiah was a faithful and honest man who had the full approval of the king.

God uses honest and trustworthy people. God chose Nehemiah because he was an honest man. As the cupbearer who tested the cup for the king, Nehemiah did not have any skills or the experience to rebuild the wall. Despite these circumstances, God still chose him. When God chooses us to participate in His plan, He does not look at our capabilities but at our attitudes.

Handong also holds honesty and faithfulness as core values in education. I would like to introduce several Handong members who are living out their lives as examples of syntropy in this age through their honesty and faithfulness.

Yong-Bum Kim (IT, class of 1996) received his acceptance letter from a large company and had to take another exam for his position. However, the exam questions were too difficult to answer. As the examiner left the room, a paper started to be passed around the room. People were cheating. This paper reached Yong-Bum as well. However, Yong-Bum was used to taking unsupervised exams under the Handong Honor Code, which was drafted by the student body as an effort to maintain the integrity of honesty. As a result, Yong-Bum left the room after submitting a blank answer sheet. A few days later, he was assigned to the department he desired and his new manager asked him,

"Why did you submit a blank answer sheet?"

"That's because I didn't know the answer."

"That's right. You shouldn't know the answer. That question was one that none of you could answer with your knowledge. It was designed to test your honesty. However, all the other people somehow managed to find similar answers."

The manager had a perky smile on his face.

To Hye-Eun Kim (Design, class of 2001), honesty was not an important virtue before she enrolled in Handong. However, during her time in Handong, she learned how important honesty was before God. After her graduation she started working for a company and practiced honesty in every aspect of her life. She rejected participating in dishonest activities such as substitute attendance, manipulating overtime hours, and false application for meal coupons. As a result, she was selected as the company's most influential employee. When selecting new employees, the company also invited her to participate as a member of the executive-level interviewing committee usually made up of the president, CEO, and board members. During important decisions such as promotions, changes in department structures and more, the management asked for her opinion. The president of the company said,

"Ms. Kim, because you are honest and your opinions always benefit the company rather than your personal gain, I can trust you with anything in our company."

"Be holy, because I am holy." (1 Peter 1:16)

The main actors of Syntropy Drama are those who have engraved honesty and faithfulness in their lives. Honesty changes the world and faithfulness moves the world.

The Rebuilder of Broken Places

Nehemiah was not only honest and faithful, but he was a praying leader. The power of prayer was the driving force to rebuild the walls of Jerusalem (which had lain abandoned for 140 years) in just 52 days. Nehemiah first offered a prayer of confession and repentance for the sins committed by the Israelites (Nehemiah 1:6-7). Instead of transferring the sin to others, he prayed a mature prayer by referring to "we" in order to embrace and acknowledge the sins as his own. Whenever he faced opposition, ridicules, mockery or threats in rebuilding the wall, he fought back with his confession of faith: God was with him and he was only rebuilding the wall in obedience to God's will as His servant.

Nehemiah reminds God of His promise (Nehemiah 1:9) and prays a prayer of dedication saying, "Lord, use me." When he prayed, he was still diligent with his responsibilities. Prayer promotes power to give best efforts, as in the case of Nehemiah, rather than giving us an excuse to be less diligent.

Nehemiah was also a servant leader who practiced self-sacrifice. When he heard the report that those who returned from exile were in great trouble and, that the walls of Jerusalem were destroyed and the gates were burnt, he did not remain in his comfortable palace in Persia. Instead, he volunteered himself by asking the king to send him as the governor of Jerusalem. As the governor, he displayed true leadership by not only giving orders, but also by physically working with his own hands in the rebuilding project.

In Nehemiah Chapter 3, the names and roles of every participant in rebuilding of the wall are recorded in detail. Every task was divided based on the section and occupation. Everyone was encouraged to participate in the project. He appointed officers for the people to work under their authority and acknowledged their achievements. We can see that he was a leader in the forefront of the project. However, his name and role are not once mentioned in the record of the builders even once. We can see that Nehemiah was a servant leader who did not boast of his presence and accomplishments.

He was also a man of integrity who realized economic justice. Despite all the ridicule, threats, slander and conspiracy, he was able to overcome all the opposition through his excellent leadership and faithful prayers that entrusted everything to God. As a result, he was able to complete the historic rebuilding of the wall in just 52 days. We can see his faith through his confession that was lifted to God after the completion of the wall:

> "So the wall was completed on the twenty-fifth of Elul, in fifty-two days. When all our enemies heard about this, all the surrounding nations were afraid and lost their self-confidence, because they realized that this work had been done with the help of our God." (Nehemiah 6:15-16)

By completing the rebuilding of the wall, which also functioned as protection from foreign invasions, Nehemiah's major assignment was finished. The hardware for spiritual revival was ready. Following this ministry, Ezra who was a priest and teacher continued the movement for spiritual revival. The book of Nehemiah records various movements of Israel's spiritual revival, such as reading the Law (chapter 8), repentance and renewal of the covenant (chapter 9), resettlement of Jerusalem (chapter 11), dedication of the temple (chapter 12), and faith and spiritual reformation (chapter 13). Nehemiah's leadership should be highlighted in two categories. First, he returned from Persia to complete his assignment (chapter 13). Secondly, he carried out his mission, reformation of faith and church. Nehemiah was an exceptional spiritual leader who not only completed the rebuilding of the wall but also succeeded in the reformation of faith and church.

The book of Nehemiah was the last historical narrative in the Old Testament. The following 400 years until the coming of Jesus Christ was a dark period where God did not speak through prophets. Through the account of the rebuilding of the wall and the spiritual revival, the book of Nehemiah demonstrates God's covenant to restore all the land through His faithfulness, love and grace.

Through studying Nehemiah's work, I discovered

the archetype of Jesus Christ who will restore the fallen world. This led me to establish the educational vision and goal of Handong to raise the 21st century global Christian leaders like Nehemiah who will bring restoration in spirituality, character, intellect and the natural world.

"Your people will rebuild the ancient ruins and will raise up the age-old foundations; you will be called Repairer of Broken Walls, Restorer of Streets with Dwellings." (Isaiah 58:12)

Study in Order to Give

Korea was once a poor country that has overcome poverty. Right after the Korean War (June 25, 1950 to July 27, 1953), it is a true miracle that a land once known as one of the poorest countries in the world has now joined the ranks of top developed countries. In just half a century, Korea has turned from a war-stricken country that received aid from developed countries to a country that is giving aid to other nations.

Koreans should never forget the help received from international organizations such as the United Nations, UNESCO, USAID, and etc. Many United Nations soldiers lost their lives during the Korean War. The following quote was written in my elementary school text book:

"This textbook is supplied with the support of UNESCO and UNKRA."

I was really thankful for using the textbooks provided by United Nation's organizations. UNKRA (the United Nations Korea Reconstruction Agency) was a special UN organization in 1950 to assist the reconstruction efforts in Korea. The dissolution of this organization took place in 1958.

After graduating from university, I completed my military service in 1967. That same year, I left for the United States with only US $150, which was the maximum exchange amount allowed for those that passed the exam to study overseas. With an extremely low gross domestic product rate, Korea faced a difficult economic situation. After 12 years in the United States, I experienced mixed feelings when I returned home as an invited scientist and professor at KAIST. It was a very different country from the one I had left 12 years ago. This time, I returned as a father of two children, and most importantly, as a born-again Christian, a new creation in Jesus Christ. The late Pastor Dong-Myoung Kim (Los Angeles Korean Baptist Church) who led our Bible studies gave me a farewell gift—a scripture frame that he personally wrote with Korean calligraphy. It said, "I am indebted." (Romans 1:14)

I was indeed indebted. I am indebted to the late Professor Norman Stoloff at Rensselaer Polytechnic Institute (RPI), in Troy, New York, who instructed me with passion. He also gave me the opportunity to study in an American university with a full scholarship as a research assistant. The scripture that Pastor Kim gave me contained many profound messages.

My father who saw the frame hung in my study room asked,

"How much debt do you have? What makes you so proud of being in debt that you are willing to write 'I am indebted' on the wall like that?"

When Handong opened its doors, I hung this frame in the prayer room in Hyundong Hall. This was because I believed that we were all indebted to the Gospel.

Therefore, the purpose and goal of our study should be for the benefit of others rather than for ourselves. We must never forget God's grace and His blessings upon our nation. Korea is scarce in natural resources and does not produce a drop of oil, but Korea experienced prosperity through the aid from developed countries. Korea must remember the countries and peoples that helped her.

One way for Handong to repay the debt as a university is to invite students from developing countries and provide them with the educational opportunities to hear the Gospel, which gives new life. Handong students are encouraged to meditate on the meaning of the academic motto, "Study in Order to Give to Others." I am convinced that each student from developing countries will become leaders who will fulfill God's Great Commission when they return to their own countries.

Handong students also study with a banner that states "Why Not Change the World?" In order to change the world, we must first change ourselves. We must live a life of humility, a life that willingly accepts disadvantages and sacrifices, and a life that strives to become more like our Lord, Jesus Christ. The world will take notice of this kind of people and will begin to wonder about them. This is true Christian leadership. This is syntropy in the realm of academics.

What Is a New Educational Framework in the 21st Century?

We now live in a complex, chaotic, and globalized world. The 21st century universities stand in a dire need of a paradigm shift, calling for a fresh revolutionary approach to education. True education is not simply conveying and transmitting knowledge, but

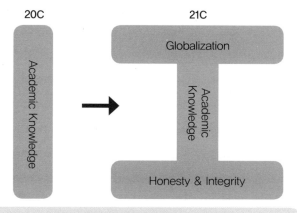

- Y 1994: Commercialization of Internet (www)
- Y 1995: Launching of the Global Economy (GATT 〉 WTO)

The shift of educational paradigms from the 20th century to the 21st century cultivating the moral, ethical and spiritual realms as well.

The middle of the 1990s was the epoch of entering into the information technology-driven global community. The commercial use of the World Wide Web (WWW) began in 1994. Then the GATT (General Agreement on Tariffs and Trade) was changed to the WTO (World Trade Organization), which gave impetus to the global economy. The opening of Handong in 1995 coincided with the opening of the 21st century IT-driven global world.

From the Industrial Age in the 20th century to the Information Age and Globalization Age in the 21st century, our education system must adapt to the changing needs of the current social environment.[23] The new educational framework that modern education must take can be depicted as the Chinese letter signifying "Engineering, 工 (pronounced, 'Gong' in Korean)," shown in the figure above.

The bottom horizontal stroke of "工" is the foundation of 'character building and spiritual training,' or to be more precise, honesty and integrity. The vertical stroke symbolizes 'Comprehensive Academic Knowledge,' while the top horizontal stroke represents 'Education to foster Globalization and Creativity.' The stability of '工' lies in its foundation because a weak foundation only weakens or destroys whatever has been built up with the accumulated education structure. Such weak foundations will ultimately harm society rather than helping it. Handong emphasizes the importance of a well-rounded '工' education more than ever before.

The following communiqué was adopted during the 2009 World Conference on Higher Education, a conference attended by key stakeholders of UNESCO members at the UNESCO headquarters in Paris.

At no time in history has it been more important to invest in higher education as a major force in building an inclusive and diverse knowledge society and to advance research, innovation, and creativity. Higher education must not only give solid skills for the present and future world but must also contribute to the education of ethical citizens committed to the construction of peace, the defense of human rights, and the values of democracy.

It is imperative to note that the UNESCO communiqué places importance on the focus of ethics and religious studies in higher education. Underlying this statement may have been the bankruptcy of the Lehman Brothers in 2008, which led to a global financial crisis. Such bankruptcy was known to be caused by the unethical behavior of those in senior management positions.

"The fear of the Lord is the beginning of knowledge, but fools despise wisdom and instruction." (Proverbs 1:7)

"Do not conform any longer to the pattern of this world, but be transformed by the renewing of your mind. Then you will be able to test and approve what God's will is - his good, pleasing and perfect will."

(Romans 12:2)

At the founding of Handong in 1995, the school established the "Handong Honor Code" to advocate the practice of integrity among its students. At Handong, all university exams are unsupervised. In addition, through a team system, students are encouraged to interact with their team professor on a personal level. Academic knowledge is transferred in the classroom, while students are able to practice character building through dormitory life where they live according to their team communities. Handong imple-

Handong opened in 1995, in Pohang, Korea

ments a residential college system in which each team professor is responsible for the spiritual and character education of the team students (non-academic).

Handong was the first Korean university to implement the enrollment of freshmen with undeclared majors. This allows students to discover their talents and potentials and to explore various majors during their first year. Furthermore, Handong has incorporated mandatory English education and IT courses to enhance the global communication ability of the students. In preparation for the future economic powers of northeast Asia, all students must enroll in either Chinese characters or a Chinese conversation course as a pre-requisite to graduate from Handong. Moreover, Handong students are required to select a multiple major to add to their diversity of knowledge which is essential to global citizens. Education should no longer remain at the level of knowledge and simply learning to read, write, or memorize. Through education based on love one another, students should be able to seek solutions for the realistic problems they face. Good solutions are not merely technical answers, political regulations, or financial aid because those are not what solve our fundamental problems. Ultimately, this is why this generation is demanding well-rounded individuals who are intelligent, but also who possess sound character and are spiritually well-grounded.

> "All Scripture is God-breathed and is useful for teaching, rebuking, correcting and training in righteousness, so that the servant of God may be thoroughly equipped for every good work." (2 Timothy 3:16-17)

From the Fall to Syntropic Education

When God created the world, He established three

fundamental relationships for man: 1) a relationship between man and God; 2) a relationship between man and man; and 3) a relationship between man and nature.[24] However, the relationships were broken due to man's disobedience which resulted in the first broken relationship with God. A broken relationship with God leads to broken relationships with others, as we become more selfish and seek to gain personal benefits, power, and materialistic goods. Much like the law of gravity, our selfish nature pulls down like a magnetic force, which draws dishonesty and greed to ourselves. God has entrusted us with the responsibility of stewardship, to rule and preserve God's created world.

This led to the Fall of Man from the God-centered state to human-centered state, and ultimately into materialism, which is the entropic phenomenon towards disorder, corruption, and death. The advancements in science and technology have destroyed the natural environment. This has led to climate change which has

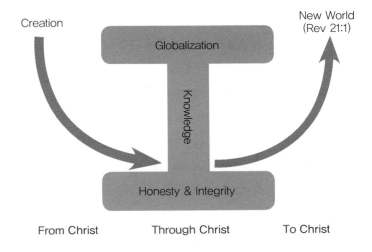

Creation

New World
(Rev 21:1)

Globalization

Knowledge

Honesty & Integrity

From Christ   Through Christ   To Christ

From the entropic fall to syntropic restoration

destroyed the ecosystem and the creation order, and eventually causing God's creation to groan in pain (Romans 8:18-23).

In Genesis 1, God's creation order was perfect, but was gradually destroyed by our sin (Genesis 3). Therefore, disorder and chaos naturally increases (entropy) and our world is gradually clouded with confusion, decadence, and disorder. The only solution to transform the fallen creation order and restore 'syntropy' in God's creation is through syntropic education. Creator and Redeemer of our Lord Jesus Christ is at the core of unfolding the Syntropy Drama.

> "For from him and through him and for him are all things. To him be the glory forever! Amen." (Romans 11:36)

The fundamental goal of Christian education is to restore and reconstruct the world's spiritual, ethical, and materialistic creation order. God has established Handong to restore the broken spiritual, moral, and intellectual world of this age by educating and training Nehemiahs of the 21st century— leaders who will not conform to the patterns of this world. To this end, Handong is conducting well-rounded (工) education to cultivate and train the global Christian leaders in the 21st century of the global community.

"Go into all the world and preach the good news to all creation." (Mark 16:15)

International Syntropic Educational Activities

The world faces global challenges, which require global solutions. These interconnected global challenges call for far-reaching changes in how we think and act for the dignity of fellow human beings. It is not enough for education to produce individuals who can read, write and count. Education must be transformative and bring shared values to life. It must cultivate an active care for the world and for those with whom we share it. Education must also be relevant in answering big questions of this day. Technological solutions, political regulation or financial instruments alone cannot achieve sustainable development. It requires transforming the way people think and act. Education must fully assume its central role in helping people to forge more just, peaceful, tolerant and inclusive societies. It must give people the understanding, skills and values such as honesty and integrity they need to cooperate in resolving the interconnected challenges of the 21st Century.

In September 2012, the Global Education First Initiative (GEFI) was also launched by the UN Secretary-General Ban Ki-moon to expand access to education, to improve the quality of learning, and to foster global citizenship. (www.globaleducationfirst.org)

In order to foster global citizenship, Handong Global University is conducting a global citizenship education for all students from its opening in March 1995 as the Handong Honor Code as following;

• The global citizen is responsible for all he or she says, does and writes;

• The global citizen is honest and diligent in his or her academic and social life; and

• The global citizen is willing to sacrifice and help others.

In order to become a global leader, one needs also global communication skills, an open-mind to understand different cultures, and professional knowledge and experience on a global scale. Handong's vision of fostering global leaders targets not only Korean students but also international students.

Although Handong does not have strong financial resources, it has continued to support international students from more than 60 countries. Many of them come from developing countries in Africa, the Middle East, Southeast Asia, and Latin America. Handong works to support these countries by providing scholarships and training the next generation leader for their respective countries.

As a result, in April 2007, Handong was designated by UNESCO[25] as a UNITWIN (University Twinning & Networking University). UNITWIN is a global networking program sponsored by UNESCO that promotes the elimination of knowledge gaps between universities through collaboration and by sharing knowledge. UNITWIN was established in 1992 with the aim of developing inter-university cooperation, while emphasizing the transfer of knowledge between universities and the promotion of academic solidarity across the world. In 2007, UNESCO appointed Handong to host the UNITWIN network program on Capacity Building of Sustainable Development in Developing Countries in the Asian Region in April 2007. Through the Handong-UNITWIN international cooperative educational program, students may enroll in the Global Enterprise Entrepreneurship (GEE) MBA program or a short-term Global Entrepreneurship Training (GET) program. These programs collaborate with 20 other universities worldwide and combine academic training in the areas of international business, technology, and international law.

To solve the global problem of poverty, United Nations Secretary - General Ban, Ki-Moon launched the UNAI (UN Academic Impact)[26] program in November 2010. UNAI aims to generate a global movement of minds to promote a new culture of intellectual social responsibility. It is animated by a commitment to certain bedrock principles, such as freedom of inquiry, opinion and speech, educational opportunity for all, global citizenship, sustainability, and dialogue. This program is a joint collaboration between the United Nations and universities worldwide with a commitment to support and advance 10 basic principles. Handong was selected as a global hub university for the fifth principle, "A commitment to building capacity in higher education systems across the world." As a UNAI global hub university, the role of Handong was to educate the next-generation leaders as global entrepreneurs, assist in reducing the knowledge gap between universities in advanced and developing nations, and research green energy for green growth.

As an activity of the UNAI global hub university, Handong made a mutual agreement with Lawrence

Livermore National Laboratory (LLNL) in December 2011. The purpose was for joint research in developing a safe and sustainable energy source: a stable, atomic-fusion energy hybrid power plant. The content of the research was later published in June 2012 under the title, "Bringing Star Power to Earth" in the *UN Chronicle* (the official news journal of the United Nations).[27]

UNAI has also created UNAI ASPIRE "Action by Students to Promote Innovation and Reform through Education." ASPIRE is a university student-driven initiative which is united in promoting UNAI's vision of institutions of higher education and research. It actively upholds its 10 universally accepted principles and thus contributes to the fulfilment of the global mandate and mission of the United Nations. In March 3, 2012, Handong organized 201 UNAI ASPIRE Korea consisting of 14 Korean universities for the purposes of enhancing mutual collaboration and of solving global issues faced by the global community.

"Peace and prosperity in the 21st century depend on increasing the capacity of people to think and work on a global and intercultural basis. As technology opens borders, educational and professional exchange opens minds."

Institute of International Education (IIE), New York. (www.iie.org)

The 21st Century Leaders in Syntropy

Young-Hwan Choi's Story

Young-Hwan Choi of Brush with Hope

CEO of Mtree, an international non-profit organization in New York

Entering class of 1999 (Communication Arts and Science)

Syntropy Project During His Service in the Military

When Young-Hwan entered his military service as an officer in the army, he was fresh out of college with a vision of becoming a world-changer. His first important task was to prepare the 60th anniversary event to commemorate the founding of the army in Korea. He began to conceptualize a musical which would allow the celebrity soldiers to exhibit their talents. Although there were a few minor problems with receiving financial support from the army headquarters, Young-Hwan decided to push through with his plan with the world-challenger mentality he had learned at Handong.

His musical was based on a true story of a colonel who had lost a leg in an effort to save a fellow soldier in a demilitarized mine field. Together with his direct supervisor, Young-Hwan convinced the officers in charge that his musical would help to convey the patriotism of the army and boost the mentality and morale of the soldiers. He succeeded in receiving a minimal amount of funds and successfully launched the first army musical, *MINE*.

Tourists from China, Japan, and Southeast Asia came to watch this musical, starring South Korean celebrities such as Kangta and Dong-Geun Yang. So many tourists came to visit that there were not enough lodging accommodations. News of the musical was widely spread, leading to road shows in Seoul, Chuncheon, Busan, Daegu, Daejeon, and Gwangju. As Young-Hwan had only a few days left prior to his discharge from the army, he voluntarily asked to postpone his discharge for an additional six more months, which was granted for the first time in the history of the Korean Army.

Milk Carton University – Creating Something from Nothing

From the front lines, cut off from all external communication, Young-Hwan once again started to visualize his dreams. One day, after drinking his daily milk, he decided to jot down on the carton (which he had cut open and dried) various questions that trouble the young people of this generation. From this idea, he established his own imaginary "Milk Carton University" and wrote to famous people, inviting them to speak on such topics at his imaginary university.

After he was discharged from the army, he gathered his military savings and embarked on a journey to personally visit the speakers of his imaginary university. In big and small ways, Young-Hwan experienced God leading him as he traveled the world. His passion and analog-communication method—as shown through the milk-carton letters—moved the hearts of the famous people to whom he had written. Finally, Young-Hwan published his *Renting Milk*

Carton University, containing answers from the famous men and women he had met, which has also moved the hearts of young people today.

Planting a Mustard Seed

During his world tour, Young-Hwan not only met famous men and women who have impacted the world but also many young people with a passion for changing the world. These young people were also excellent leaders in each of their own professions. Young-Hwan knew that such precious opportunities should not be wasted. He began his own network of people who ultimately became his partners at Mtree. In 2009, young Koreans came together in New York for the founding of Mtree.

Mtree stands for Mustard Tree, a cultural ministry run purely on talent donations by second-generation Koreans to spread the Gospel in Africa. Sixty years ago, Korea was war-torn and one of the poorest countries in the world; it had to depend on foreign aid for survival. Now, they wanted to give back more than just food or medical supplies by helping young people to dream dreams and build their own future.

Under the name, "Brush with Hope," Young-Hwan opened an exhibition in a gallery in Chelsea, New York with artwork drawn by African children. For this program, many young Korean artists travelled to Africa to provide free art classes. African boys and girls, who had never been given the opportunity to express themselves through color, started to "Brush with Hope." These works of art were transported back to New York and received wide attention during the exhibition. New Yorkers, living the up-style life but feeling empty and futile on the inside, were encouraged by the art work of the African children, who were living on barely one meal a day. This exhibition continued for two consecutive years in New York and is currently under plans for a worldwide exhibition tour. The Mtree project is not limited to art, but is gradually expanding to the areas of fashion design, sand sculpture, and opera.

In the words of Young-Hwan:

There are so many children in Africa who are deprived of cultural benefits. I want to go and help develop their talents while spreading the Gospel of Jesus to these children. At first, these children did not even know what a brush was—and some even tried to eat the brush—but now are able to draw their own art work. That in itself is touching, but even deeper than that, is seeing these children questioning themselves about what their dreams are, and expressing their dreams on paper. That is when these children start to see the world in a different light. That is when they are able to discover the talents that God has given them.

The Handong mentality of "Why not change the world? Why not benefit others by studying?" made Young-Hwan's dream possible, and that dream is now achieving miracles in the world.

"He said to them, 'Go into all the world and preach the gospel to all creation.'" (Mark 16:15)

Hyoung-Soo Kim's Story

CEO of Tree Planet, a global social enterprise

Entering class of 2006 (Communication Arts and Science)

Tree Planet to combat desertification

Syntropy Projects to Save Nature

Tree Planet CEO Hyoung-Soo Kim is an active environmental conservationist who works through his tree-planting mobile application. His app was selected as an official app at G20 2010 Seoul and the United Nations Convention to Combat Desertification (UNC-CD). (www.treepla.net)

Hyoung-Soo Kim of Tree Planet

In the words of Hyung-Soo :

I am standing where I am now, and Tree Planet is where it is now because of the Handong slogan, "Why Not Change the World?" It was that vision embodied by the slogan that challenged me to change my values and ultimately became the seed of Tree Planet.

I have always been interested in environmental issues. Ever since my first documentary on environmental-awareness that I produced in high school, I have put a lot of effort into capturing my philosophy on environmental protection. Studying at Handong provided me with a background in liberal arts connecting various disciplines. Furthermore, the deep blue waters of Donghae (the East Sea of Korea), the rich greens of the conifer forests, and the magnificent reservoir adjacent to HGU campus that make up Handong's geographic surroundings were a blessing for me. It was several years of incomparable firsthand experience on the benefits of the environment. It was vital to my establishing a value of coexistence with the environment.

I took academic leave in my junior year and enlisted in the military service. During my service, I spent my spare time planning a project for a smartphone application that will result in an actual tree being planted somewhere on the earth. One day, God provided me with a comrade as I was sharing my vision with a junior ranking soldier. He liked my ideas and started to discuss practical project plans with me.

Every evenings after completing my duties for the

day, I would crouch down in bed with a felt blanket over my head to work on the business plan while the rest of my platoon went to sleep. I even tended a small garden to gain insight into arboriculture. I also kept my eyes open for a partner.

As a result, Tree Planet was born after I was released from army service. Today, more than 650,000 people around the world have planted about 450,000 trees in Korea and six other countries including Mongolia, Indonesia, various African countries, and China. The trees have been planted to form 24 actual forests. Tree Planet's revenue structure is straight forward. App users are automatically encouraged to plant a tree within the app and take care of the planted tree with sunshine from the sun and water from a watering can. The sun is branded with the logo of a particular business, which in turns pays to plant a tree when certain conditions are met. The company benefits from brand exposure and an eco-friendly corporate image.

Jun-Hee Ahn's Story

CEO of Hand Studio, a Smart TV contents producing company

Entering class of 2001 (Management and Economics)

Hand Studio to make a world-changing corporate culture

I was a 20-year old freshman the very first time I stood on the subway platform, waiting for the train to come in. I recall it was the day before leaving to China for a short-term mission. I had just come to Seoul, and a friend had provided me with a place to lay my head down for the night before leaving for the airport the next day. My friend, who knew that I had never boarded a subway train before, said in good humor, "Jun-Hee, don't forget to take off your shoes before boarding the subway." Although it was an obvious jest, the momentary hesitation and uncertainty that overcame me are clear to me today as it was many years ago.

On the subway, I was fascinated and curious. My gaze darting to and fro. It was then that my eyes fell upon a man who laboriously made his way into the car we were on. He was disabled, with both legs amputated. The man cleared his throat and began crying out to the other passengers, "I lost both my legs in an accident. I need your help to make it through the day." Nobody helped him. I plucked up my courage and looked to my friend to suggest we help the man. My friend nodded in consent. We pulled out a couple thousand Korean Won (about US$2) from our pockets and handed it to him, saying "take heart." The man ignored the cash and instead clenched my wrist.

"Young man," he said, "money comes later. Could I ask for your audience? I have a story to tell."

Without saying a word, I sat down before him and started to listen to his story. The man told me he lost both his legs in an accident at a construction site. When he regained his consciousness from the accident on a hospital bed, both his legs had been amputated. Later, his wife abandoned him and took their young son. He was alone with his widowed mother. Suicide was always on his mind, but it was his responsibility to his mother that spurred him to seek training and find work in a factory. The factory job did not last long. After frequent mistreatments from the factory owner and delayed wages, the man left the factory and looked for a place to end his life. Betrayed by life and denied by expectations, he cut his wrists. His life was not to be extinguished, and once again he gained consciousness. Still unable to find reason or motivation to live on, the man lay idle in futility. It was his responsibility for his mother that forced him back to his feet and out to the Seoul metropolitan subway. It was his first day, and I was the first person to listen to him.

There was nothing I could say that would be of any consolation, so I blurted out, "Mister, when I grow up, I'll make a world where hard-working people like you get treated justly. I promise you. I have nothing to offer, but I believe in Jesus, and I will pray for you." The man quietly folded his hands together, and I prayed for him, both of us sitting on the floor of the car in Subway Line 1. I kept on meditating on the promise I had just made. My friend and I missed our station, and it was only after my friend nudged me that I grabbed my bag on the luggage rack and hastily got off the subway, saying farewell to the man. The last look of his face was in tears, with his arms open to the heavens, shouting "I'm going to live on, I must live on."

A Promise to 'Make a New World'

A decade has passed since that fateful meeting.

Hand Studio, the company that I built, allows employees freedom to conduct personal business without having to request leave, paid or otherwise. Once a month, no matter how busy, all our employees drop everything and go on an outing. To the younger employees with an upcoming wedding, we give a congratulatory donation of 10 million Korean Won (about US$10,000). The employees are neither evaluated nor discriminated on grounds of academic background, hometown, or appearances. Both long-time staff members and incoming staff members are evaluated solely by their level of skill and effort. At Hand Studio, we can proudly say that everybody is given equal opportunity.

Each full-time employee of Hand Studio sponsors a disadvantaged child. Every year at the end of the year party, the company invites and pays for the travel fees for all the parents of employees, whether they are in Korea, China, or Japan, to spend time with us in the best hotel in Seoul.

The promise I made to the man on the subway 10 years ago, "I'll make a world where everyone gets equal opportunity" became the very reason and vision for Hand Studio. We are building a company where there is no discrimination, and just compensation is given to hard work and effort.

Practicing What I Learned!

I often get asked how I came to build a company like this. I always answer, "I practice what I learned."

From Handong, I learned five prerequisites to becoming a world-changing leader. I merely try my best to practice those requisites that I have been taught. They are as follows:

I have a banner I can wave. Through my life in Handong, I learned to look to God. He is the One I strive to please. "Why Not Change the World?" is a phrase we hear all too frequently in Handong. When I accepted that God was an absolute being and I existed for His will, I found courage and the means to achieve that motto. In my four years at Handong, not a single day passed by without my sincerest sharing of God's great will. At Hand Studio, employee ID cards do not include information on department or rank. Instead, the cards have a picture of the cardholder's vision. I discovered how important it was to embrace a dream, an ideal that can make or break a person. I introduced the idea of the ID cards as a device to share my secret in life with our employees.

Second, I have an unfailing conviction. Handong taught me the virtues of honesty and diligence. God's words in the Bible taught me to never compromise honesty. We pledge ourselves to honest and diligent work. Major corporations come to us, even without any solicitations or lobbying. Hand Studio is currently an industry leader, with sales growth every year. We are also ranked first among "remarkable companies."

Third, I have a mentor I can follow for a lifetime. President Young-Gil Kim dedicated his life to educating leaders after God's own heart. A leader with a banner and unfaltering conviction, President Kim could not be a better role model as a forerunner and CEO. Sometimes we come across seemingly endless challenges, hardships, temptations and discouragements. There are times when we give our best and passionately exhaust everything at our disposal, only to discover it just is not enough. Whenever I experience such shortcomings, I look to the life of President Kim and to Handong Global University, and it fills me with indescribable peace. The nebulous fear vanishes before a great life of faith, conviction, and a dream for an ideal. My role model spared words, and instead chose to walk the path for 20 years. What excuse would I have before him?

Fourth, I have a lifelong friend. Hand Studio was built on the unfailing trust of a friend I made in Handong. The seed money I needed was about 100 million Korean Won (about US$100,000), but even with everything I saved from my last job, I could only reach half that amount. There was a particular friend from

Handong that I had shared my dream with. We used to talk about creating an exemplary business in the near future. I sought him and handed him a copy of the business plan, enthusiastically describing how I would achieve the details in the plan. My friend stopped me half-way through the presentation and without hesitation, pulled out a bankbook from the shelf and slid it over to me.

"This is everything I have saved. Jun-Hee, I want you to use it with me to start a business of our dreams."

Looking at my awestruck face, my friend explained, "I remember that vision you told me when we were students at Handong. I haven't forgotten how earnestly you wanted to create an outstanding business together. This is your chance, and I think you should take it first."

I understood, and I could not hold back the gushing tears. It was a great blessing to have a friend who placed unwavering faith and trust in me. That was how Hand Studio first got off the ground, with a generous donation from a friend. Through the tuition of dreams, Hand Studio (the merriest corporation in the world) came to be.

Last but not least, I have an anthem. "Here we gather to follow the Lord, we stand here with our hands held high, and He guides us and leads us. He moves here in Handong Global University" is the first stanza of the "Handong Song". The melody and lyrics always set our heart ablaze, looking back at all the friendships and values we established together. I dream of another song, a new chapter if you will. As all the Handongians here at Hand Studio agree, I hope to hear another song, that of beautiful stories with which we can all empathize and sing along with. Following the dreams, ideals, and values instilled by our time at Handong, the path paved by our professors, and the trust of our friends, I have no doubt that the tunes we were taught at Handong will one day be heard in resounding fashion throughout the world.

Once a simple student from the rural areas, I believe it was by the Lord's good grace that I came to be a student at Handong. Upon that grace, I look forward to another day in the company of outstanding excellence, honesty, diligence, and happiness. Praise the Lord, and "Why not change the world?!"

Chapter 4

Syntropy Christian Leadership

A Path a Christian Leader Must Take

I first picked up Henri Nouwen's book *In the Name of Jesus*, in 2005. It has been a book I have greatly enjoyed over the years. There are many books in the world about leadership, but I believe that this particular book is the only one that deals with supreme leadership that puts spirituality as its foundation. The book promotes a leadership that does not just improve from "Good to Great," but from "Good to Supreme." If a "Good to Great" leadership aims to achieve personal goals in the secular world, a "Good to Supreme" leadership is on a different higher level in that it aims to achieve the will of our Sovereign Creator God.

I believe that this book serves to illustrate a blueprint for a new kind of syntropy restoring order where there is disorder in a world where entropy is increasing. God had originally designed this world to be a beautiful place. I re-read *In the Name of Jesus* this summer and meditated on some key values that I deemed appropriate to Christian leadership.

Henri Nouwen emphasizes that a leader must give up the desire for power and live humbly through prayer and forgiveness. However, so many leaders are greedy for popularity and power. I am not exempt from this either. God wants us to live a life of prayer instead of being focused on things; a life of ministering instead of wanting popularity; and a life guided by Him instead of trying to be the guide. He wants us to be leaders who pray continuously, leaders who always trust Him, and leaders that offer up our weaknesses to Him. Let me elaborate.

A true Christian leader must first, through prayer, reside in the knowledge of God's love. One must know within the core of one's being, the reason of his or her existence in God's love. We must reside in Jesus who asks, "Do you love me?" Henri Nouwen calls this the training of "meditative prayer."

Meditative prayer helps us avoid the vice of becoming desensitized to God's heart due to the busy things this world has to offer. Meditative prayer frees us from this world and helps us find refuge in Christ. It gives us confirmation that we already reside in God.

The word "theology" originally had a meaning of "being one with God." However, over the years theology has developed into a different meaning in the academic realm. Many say it is actually more difficult for students of theology to candidly pray to God. A true Christian leader surpasses all the rules and principles of this world and plants his roots in the spiritual and close relationship with Jesus Christ. In order to be restored, one must accept God's Word and His Word must be proclaimed once again.

Second, a true Christian leader must reject the attitude that he or she can achieve anything without God One must be humble.

The world does not listen to Jesus, nor do they pay attention to Him. Thus, the world crucifies Christ on the cross even today. In a world where power, domination, and efficiency are important values, Jesus' love is being rejected every day. Instead a true Christian leader must be a person who truly understands the love and humility of Christ who has come down to this earth.

We must be able to acknowledge our weaknesses to God and be humble in all worldly achievements. One must be able to love his or her neighbor without self-seeking interest. Jesus came to this world is to save us and to show everyone this divine love.

Third, a Christian leader must be able to willingly serve anywhere—whether in remote areas or in your own neighborhoods and whether in uncomfortable regions far away or in your local homeless shelters just down the street. In order to achieve God's will, suffering may and will follow because "uncomfortableness" is anything that puts one outside of a comfort zone. Maturity means being able to follow Him, even in places where one does not want to go.

> "Very truly I tell you, when you were younger you dressed yourself and went where you wanted; but when you are old you will stretch out your hands, and someone else will dress you and lead you where you do not want to go." (John 21:18)

This was the verse that guided me 19 years ago when I received my calling to Handong Global University. The path of a Christian leader is not like that of leaders of this world. It is not a path that keeps getting better; it is a path that leads to more and more difficult situations and ultimately ends up at the cross. The traits of Christian leadership are not characterized by strength or dominance. It is leadership of power-lessness that was demonstrated by Jesus, God's servant. This means being willing to give up worldly power and securing positions because of our love towards Jesus Christ. This is true spiritual leadership.

Eight months before Handong Global University was launched, the foundation of the University was unsettled by a huge industrial accident. The future of Handong did not look too promising. During that time, my human nature did not want to give up the secure professorship position I had in KAIST. However, God's calling strengthened me. Soon after, I became involved in countless legal actions and lawsuits. During those times, I was able to learn from Jesus Christ by meditating on the humility of the One who had obeyed God, even to His death on the cross.

Acquiring powerlessness and humility do not mean being pushed around by other people. Christian leadership does not mean mental weakness, but rather, it means giving up power because of Christ's love.

A Christian leader is in love with Jesus and is willing to follow Jesus' guidance, experiencing a rich life in Jesus Christ. Worldly people cannot understand this kind of peace.

Fourth, a Christian leader should be poor. God does not call all His leaders to financial poverty. Financial poverty is not required for Christian leadership. If so, what are the benefits of being poor? None! Being poor merely helps us become a follower instead of a leader. Financial prosperity could hinder one's discernment in identifying Jesus' will.

Handong Global University, even before its beginnings, experienced financial difficulties. Even today, Handong Global University is not that well off financially. If we are to adhere to this world's managerial principles, we have to increase the number of students. But in order to keep our identity as God's university and for a better education focused on the students' character, we are currently only accepting about 900 students each year.

Ironically, Handong is able to remain as God's university because of the financial hardships we experienced. If Handong is financially challenged due to God's will, then does that mean there is no hope for us in the future? No! It means we rely on God's provision continuously. This is even truer because it is not a man who leads this school, but God. Over the years, we have experienced many miracles through the supporters of the Papyrus Basket in Korea and overseas. Through our financial difficulties, Handong has learned to solely depend on God. I remember once telling my wife, "The fact that Handong is so poor, is a miracle. We have excellent professors, smart students, and a good educational program. Do you think we would depend on God if we were rich, on top of that? That is why poorness is a blessing, too."

My wife's response was, "You keep saying that being poor is a blessing. That is why our school never has any money. Never say such words again, dear."

When we obey Him even in the midst of financial difficulties, then we are able to learn how to be satisfied in any given situation. If we are rich, it may lead us to disobey Jesus.

> "Those who want to get rich fall into temptation and a trap and into many foolish and harmful desires that plunge people into ruin and destruction." (1 Timothy 6:9)

Agur from the book of Proverbs prayed,

> "Two things I ask of you, Lord; do not refuse me before I die: Keep falsehood and lies far from me; give me neither poverty nor riches, but give me only my daily bread." (Proverbs 30:7-8)

Fifth, a Christian leader must receive God's guidance through studying and meditating on God's Word. To practice biblical meditation means to understand God's faithfulness and guidance by meditating on the things that are in Jesus' heart in our everyday lives. A true Christian leader must think, speak, and act in Jesus' name. Jesus saved man from his own sins and came down to this earth to lead us to eternal life. A leader must be able to discern how God works in the history of mankind. He or she must be sensitive to how God leads through personal, communal, national, and international events. Through this, we are ultimately led to the cross and to our salvation.

A Christian leader's responsibility does not end in solving the problems and sufferings of this age. He or she must find and proclaim the method of how God led the Israelites out of Egypt, passed through the desert, and into the Promised Land, Canaan. Christian leaders also have a huge responsibility of understanding personal worries, familial problems, national disasters, and international conflicts through God's eyes and in faith. Even the smallest of events should be seen through the Word of God. The leader must truly believe and proclaim that through this experience one can experience Jesus' guidance.

A Christian leader must know what is in God's

heart. Through prayer and meditation, a leader must be able to present the history of God's salvation which He shows through our day's events. Continuous reading of the Scripture helps us realize where it is that we came from and where it is that we are being led.

Christian leadership needs to be a biblical servant-leadership. This cannot be just an intellectual training. It requires a deep spiritual formation involving the whole person—body, mind, and spirit. Christian leaders need to be formed in the mind of Christ, who did not cling to power but emptied himself and taking the form of a servant. Everything in our competitive and ambitious world pushes against that idea. But to the degree that such formation is being sought for and realized, there is hope for the Christian leadership of the 21st century.

Epilogue

"You are worthy, our Lord and God, to receive glory and honor and power, for you created all things, and by your will they were created and have their being." (Revelation 4:11)

This year marks the 19th year anniversary of Handong Global University. It is also the 40th year since I accepted Jesus Christ as my personal Lord and Savior. Since I accepted Christ during my employment with NASA in 1974, there have been many changes within my family. God used me to be a vessel to lead my family members to Christ. Even in my work place, God used me as a catalyst for the Syntropy Drama which is still unfolding.

Recently, I looked back at the 20 years of my life

in Handong. The moment when I was nominated as the president of Handong in April 1994; the moment when I wore the Handong shirt and welcomed the charter students at the entrance of Creation Hall in March 1995; the moment when I had to lay to rest Kyung-Sik Kang and Young-Min Kwon (two charter students who lost their lives during their Fiji mission trip); the moment when I spent 53 days in prison singing the song "Sound of Love Bell" and revising its lyrics to "Sound of Handong Bell." These are some of the countless memorable moments that I had in Handong. Remembering God's help in leading the Handong community in each step through my journey, I could not help but thank Him for His endless love and grace.

There was not a single day that passed by in Handong without financial difficulties. As God gave the Israelites manna and quail and made water gush out from the rocks, He let us experience His glory and countless miracles which continues today. Not only that, but over the past years, I have experienced countless oppositions from both the outside and the inside of the school. Actually the opposition from the outside was bearable, but it was the opposition from the inside that I found most painful. Every time fear tried to overcome me, I held onto His Word.

"But now, this is what the Lord says— he who created you, Jacob, he who formed you, Israel: Do not fear, for I have redeemed you; I have summoned you by name; you are mine. When you pass through the waters, I will be with you; and when you pass through the rivers, they will not sweep over you. When you walk through the fire, you will not be burned; the flames will not set you ablaze." (Isaiah 43:1–2)

Whenever I faced financial difficulty I held onto Philippians 4:19, "And my God will meet all your needs according to the riches of his glory in Christ Jesus."

Whenever I faced sufferings and trials God consoled me with these words, "I consider that our present sufferings are not worth comparing with the glory that will be revealed in us." (Romans 8:18)

It is God, our Creator who takes command of our lives, whether it be in times of difficulties, peace, or trials. If Jesus was not my Lord, I would not have been able to experience God's love or understand the secrets of Creation, nor would I have been able to participate in the Syntropy Drama. We, who all received His calling can be heroes in the Syntropy Drama of our own personal lives, within our families, in our workplace, and in the world.

"And the things you have heard me say in the presence of many witnesses entrust to reliable people who will also be qualified to teach others." (2 Timothy 2:2)

I expect God to pour out new dreams, hopes, and amazing grace to Handong Global University, which will be the center stage for His Syntropy Drama. This will be so because of the tears He sheds for this fallen generation. Handong still has a long way to go, but one thing that will not change is that Handong will cultivate God's leaders who will bring about change in this world. I pray that Handong will become the source of the Syntropy Drama and His water of life will flow into the desolate corners of the world. I also pray that our university will be able to maintain our identity as God's university, while turning our eyes only upon Jesus.

Furthermore, I truly hope that this syntropic movement will spread not only in Korea, but also to the rest of the world. We are all stewards of God's kingdom. I pray that Christians will be able to become leaders of this age, just like Nehemiah who rebuilt the wall from ashes.

"Remember me with favor, my God." (Nehemiah 13:31)

We are now living in the terminal generation of a chaotic, disordered, loveless and godless world of the 21st century. There are many signs of the last days as said in the Scripture of 2 Timothy 3:1-5:

"But mark this: There will be terrible times in the last days. People will be lovers of themselves, lovers of money, boastful, proud, abusive, disobedient to their parents, ungrateful, unholy, without love, unforgiving, slanderous, without self-control, brutal, not lovers of the good, treacherous, rash, conceited, lovers of pleasure rather than lovers of God— having a form of godliness but denying its power. Have nothing to do with such people."

God created the beautiful universe in the beginning, but we human beings disobeyed Him and corrupted the world through our sins. Nevertheless, God planned to restore the corrupt world through His love by sending His only begotten Son into the world (John 3:16). He wants to restore His created order for a new heaven and a new earth (Revelation 21:1). By His grace, we Christians are called as special agents for God's amazing restoration project of this fallen world through His love! Hallelujah!

The ultimate purpose of the Syntropy Drama is to transform from this entropic disordered chaotic world to the restoration of God's created order of spirituality, morality, and true life through the power of the Holy Spirit.

The centrum of the Syntropy Drama is our Lord Jesus Christ. Hallelujah!

March 2014
Young-Gil Kim

References

1) All Bible citations come from the New International Version (NIV).

2) Young-Gil Kim, *See the Invisible, Change the World* (Xulon Press, 2006).

3) Henri J. M. Nouwen, *In the Name of Jesus: Reflections on Christian Leadership* (New York: The Crossroad Publishing Company, 1992).

4) Clausius Rudolf, "On the Motive Power of Heat and on the Laws Which Can Be Deduced from it

for the Theory of Heat", *Poggendorff's Annalen der Physick LXXIX*, (March-April 1850).

5) Luigi Fantappiè, *Principi di una teoria unitaria del mondo fisico e biologico*, Humanitas Nova Editrice

(Rome, 1944).

6) Albert Szent-Gyorgyi, "Drive in Living Matter to Perfect Itself," *Synthesis* 1, No. 1 (1977): 14-26.

7) Antonella Vannini, "Entropy and Syntropy: From Mechanical to Life Science," *NeuroQuantology 2* (2005):

88–110.

8) Ulisse Di Corpo and A. Vannini, "Syntropy, the Law of Complementarity and Unity," *Syntropy 1* (2013): 83–92.

9) Philip Yancey, *What's So Amazing About Grace?* (Grand Rapids, MI: Zondervan, 2002).

10) Lindsey Hal, *The Liberation of Planet Earth* (Grand Rapids, MI: Zondervan,1974).

11) Phyllis Young-Ae Kim, *The Papyrus Basket* (Xulon Press, 2006).

12) Henry Madison Morris, *Scientific Creationism* (El Cajon, CA: Master Books, 1974).

13) *Science* 210 (November 1980): 883–887 .

14) R. Buvet and C. Ponnamperuma, eds, *Chemical Evolution and the Origin of Life* (North-Holland Publishing & American Elsevier, 1971).

15) Thomas A. Kempis, *The Imitation of Christ* (Milwaukee: Bruce Publishing Company, 1940).

16) Philip Yancey, *Rumors of Another World* (Grand

Rapids, MI: Zondervan, 2003).

17) Paul E. Little and James F. Nyquist, *Know Why You Believe* (Downers Grove, IL: IVP Books, 2008).

18) Lee Strobel, *The Case For A Creator* (Grand Rapids, MI: Zondervan, 2005).

19) Jong-Hee Han, *Modern Philosophy and Theology* (Seoul: Korea Seminary, 2006).

20) Philip Yancey, *What's So Amazing About Grace?* (Grand Rapids, MI: Zondervan, 2002).

21) Rick Warren, *The Purpose Driven Life*, 1st ed. (Grand Rapids, MI: Zondervan, 2002).

22) Charles Colson, et al., *How Now Shall We Live?* (Wheaton, IL: Tyndale House Publishers, 2004).

23) Young–Gil Kim, "A Shift of Higher Educational Paradigm with Scientific Development from Isolation to Integrative/Holistic Global Education in the 21 Century,"

Educational Research 4, (May 2010): 75–87 www.interesjournals.org/ER.

24) John Stott, *The Radical Disciple: Some Neglected Aspects of Our Calling* (Downers Grove, IL: IVP Books, 2010).

25) www.unesco.org (United Nations Education Science & Cultural Organization).

26) www.academicimpact.org (United Nations Academic Impact).

27) Young–Gil Kim, "Bringing Star Power to Earth," *UN Chronicle*, No. 1&2, (2012): 47-49.